MINDFUL RESONANCE

An introduction
to the seven frequencies
for holistic healing
and meditation.

BY CHRISTELLE CHOPARD

This book reflects the views and personal experience of the author. This book is not intended as a guide to independent self-healing or therapy. If you have any specific questions, or insights you like to share, contact the institute at: info@dharmi.com.

This book is dedicated...

to you

to the wise teachers who have crossed my path

to Amarun.

OVERVIEW

INTRODUCTION

Dharmi® Vortex of Energy

An Active Meditation.

A unique experience honoring our constant evolution.

A GPS for our soul to follow our journey with clarity, harmony, and integrity!

This practice, and Meditation does not qualify as therapy, nor is any of this information designed to be medical, or clinical advice. If you have health or psychological issues, we recommend that you see a doctor or psychologist immediately. That being said, this information is shared with you unconditionally, but you must take full responsibility for your decisions, and make use of the techniques and tools we have offered.

What are the fundamental aspects that are considered in the Vortex of Energy Meditation? Many ways and forms are combined in this Meditation. Like the pieces of a puzzle, they come together for an integral and fulfilling experience. In this book, you will receive an introduction to the main aspects that are taken into consideration and taught through this simple, yet profound experience.

1. The main intention is to balance your frequency, or vibration with clear intention. This is done by aligning your intention with the Five Elements and Seven Frequencies. Collectively, these form the framework of your inner world, which is in constant movement. They are influenced by your surroundings, your environment, and your own response mechanism.

2. Sacred Geometry will provide an understanding about the laws of the universe, and how we can apply them for our balance and well-being.

3. Qigong and the Dantiens are key aspects to channeling, activating, and directing the vital energy. The three Dantiens are the Navel (the Golden Stove), the Heart, and the Third Eye.

4. The Sushumna and the Chakras are the central line of the torus(*).

5. The breath and bandhas are key aspects to binding and containing your energy. The four bandhas are Mula Bandha, Uddiyana Bandha, Jalandhara Bandha, and Maha Bandha.

6. Meditation and intention become part of your life.

The Origin of My Quest

Since childhood I've been familiar with the language of nature. One day, my grand mother told me a story of her youth. While returning home on a bicycle, she saw a map in the sky. She read that World War II had ended, and that new country boundaries would be created in Europe. Arriving home, she immediately shared this message with her parents. They turned on the radio; a news flash announced the end of the war, and the creation of new frontiers. After hearing this story, I asked the universe to send me such signs. I started studying, looking for answers to find my own way of life; my purpose and my mission. As a teenager, gently laying my hands on my mother's back, I relieved the intense pain caused by a herniated disc from which she suffered. From that time on, I started to wonder about this apparent power that I had, an energy which afforded others relief of pain through the use of my hands.

For years, I have sought, explored, and studied holistic and alternative therapies. I found that the basis of everything is simply a case of letting go of the ego, which allows us to completely open up to love, and to channel the energy and light, without judgment or expectation. It seems simple at first, but it is difficult to apply. To learn more, and to understand this phenomenon, I studied and practiced many methods of healing, therapy, and holistic treatment.

Starting in 1991, I looked back over everything I had learned, and recognized certain patterns in my own life. I used this knowledge to make my way through the Grinberg™ method, a therapy which helped me to heal the traumas of my childhood. With this method, I could lay the foundation, to focus, and to begin to find myself. During my continued studies, I discovered the Five Elements (Earth, Water, Fire, Air and Ether), and how they are integrated in a holistic therapeutic process. During that time, I explored other modalities as well. I discovered it was important for me to have discipline, including moments of reflection. I also began to understand that I must adopt a spiritual practice around my eating, drinking, exercising and breathing. Indeed, good discipline creates a healthy balance both in your relationship with yourself, as well as one with those around you.

I have always been guided in my search for the keys to well-being in everyday life, and ways to inspire a better world for myself, and all my fellowmen. It can be challenging when we assume our own responsibilities and face reality, but it is also liberating.

The Exploration of Multiple Paths Through Six Continents

At age 24, I was eager to learn more, and my quest turned into an exploration of different techniques for healing and rituals performed in other cultures and traditions. I traveled in five continents finding more balance, well-being, and clarity through direct life experiences.

My adventurous temperament led me around the world. These trips have given me the opportunity to explore many paths, traditions, sciences, cultures and perspectives. Travel allowed me to expand my horizons, and taught me about sharing my knowledge with many different types of people who crossed my path. My search has led me to the four corners of the earth on a journey filled with beauty, discoveries, many challenges, and unique people.

People from all walks of life, regardless of their language, culture, social status and life circumstance can benefit from a holistic, dharmic approach, an approach that is based on life principles. This GPS for life has supported women in a shelter helping them to heal, find compassion, and the confidence to rebuild themselves. Artists, actors or performers moving through a career transition, or other kinds of artistic expression, have completed cycles to reconnect with their source of inspiration that has allowed them to move forward towards new projects with abundance.

I have had the opportunity and privilege to work both ends of the spectrum and many things in between, from large hotels, to tiny huts, and meeting people from all walks of life. In South America, I was frequently asked to appear on television shows to share inspiration. I've taught seminars in remote locations; sacred mountains and valleys in the Andes, as well as at conventions in five stars hotels. I've had the opportunity to participate in rituals held in remote locations with shamans from a different path, volunteer in shelters, to working with celebrities in their luxury homes. At other opportunities, I have participated in coaching and innovative healing methodologies based on advanced scientific research. My quest to share my knowledge, experience and to support others on their journey has been a colorful rainbow of experiences and encounters. This makes me see that I still have so much to learn and to discover.

These trips have been an opportunity to learn multiple methods, and to adapt my knowledge and approach to many different people, cultures and circumstances. Learning the practice of Qigong has brought me strength and new clarity. Tai Chi was a similar experience with many benefits; the different movements awakened new potential in me and freed my energy towards harmony. I was introduced to Buddhism and Hinduism during my time in Asia, and the practice of yoga has added to my sense of unity and integrity. Dances, both sacred and therapeutic in Asia, Australia and South America have enriched me. Their beauty has inspired and guided me towards a more balanced feminine energy within me. I underwent several experiences with shamanism in the Americas and Europe. Each one in turn, has given me a new perspective on life.

In 2003, after a decade of incredible journey around the world, without fixed address, I made the choice to return to society. I brought with me the wisdom of all those experiences and teachings, and created my company in Florida. I dedicated myself to holistic development, based on the Five Elements, the Map and the DHARMI process so that I may help others follow the ways of well-being with mindfulness.

I furthered my studies and training in various holistic therapies including Yoga, Qigong, Cranio Sacral Therapy and Graphology. I continued to explore other cultures through rewarding travels in Egypt, Arizona, Spain (the Santiago de Compostela path), and Israel, the Holy Land. The intense energy present in the streets of Jerusalem was both a strong and liberating experience.

How to Integrate Many Disciplines and Put Them into Practice in Our Daily Lives

These meditations, traditions and spiritual teachings have a real impact on our lives. Mastering them guides us to clarify our intention and our thoughts in our everyday life.

We need moments to share with our family and our friends. We must work and organize and take care of our property. In short, we must meet our needs as humans. Our energy disperses over our activities, our encounters and our experiences. Our reactions are dependent on internal and external pressures. We therefore end up losing sight of our values and our intentions under the accumulation of constraints. There are many good excuses for forgetting our positive thoughts and for staying in our centered space; a conflict in a relationship, a professional problem, the scramble of caring for children or our elderly parents, or the bills we must pay. Everything can distract us from our balance, well-being and heart center, bringing stress into our lives, and a sense of duality.

I had to resist distracting myself, as I explored the tenuous border that separates the world of our inner being from the vital integration with the outside world. Alas, sometimes we detach ourselves from our own needs, feelings and inspirations, to meet the expectations of those around us, thinking we need to do so to ensure our own survival, so intertwined are we with our relationships.

On the other hand, people who are able to listen to their own gifts, desires and inspirations, are much more integrated within themselves, and have better relationships with those around them. It is possible to respect our values, to follow our own truth, and prosper in today's society, while remaining in harmony with our surroundings. I believe that our passage in this life is to learn how to bridge these so we may express our authenticity, and share our gifts with those around us. To deal with exceedingly strong pressures, we need a stronger, clearer inner strength, allowing us to live in a space of abundance, confidence, heart and mindfulness. It is therefore essential to find harmony between our deep inspirations, and the requirements of our direct environment. Over time, the interplay between all these disciplines has become obvious to me. I have tried to create a language translating these philosophies in a way that can be accessible and practical in our life. I wish to contribute to the fulfillment of harmony between our deep aspirations and the outside world. I have therefore translated these many spiritual teachings to make a coherent daily practice for the 21st century. The DHARMI Method is a real synthesis of this work, which guides our steps on the path of life. It is life and business coaching based on holistic research and the fundamental law of nature.

Everything in life is related to resonance, perspective and vibration. Every word, every action, every relationship is sacred. The word DHARMI seemed to me to be a symbol to share and support personal development. I have been inspired by this brand name to symbolize the transition from life experiences (karma), towards wisdom and a path of righteousness (dharma). It was later that I learned that "dharmi" in Hindi, means "sacred".

The DHARMI Method is a guide for our daily lives. This Method is a holistic approach based on positive intentions and wholesome values. It considers our spaces of reflection, our inspiration, our needs, and our relationships. When you take a moment to clarify your thoughts and align yourself with the resonance of a positive intention, it changes your mindset and your perspective. This Map revolves around guidelines and benchmarks to clarify thoughts, actions, reactions, emotions and objectives. It guides you in your quest and your intention, and empowers a new awakening at every stage of life. The Method is based on three pathways and Maps based on the Five Elements. Each of the paths can be followed independently. However, the integration of the three paths in the Method leads to full holistic development.

Cycle of Evolution

The Cycle of Evolution is a holistic and integral portal consisting of five steps to managing stress and clearing any obstacles that are restricting you. This process helps you to access your being through an area of clarification to find authentic expression. (Reference: Book "Cycle of Evolution".)

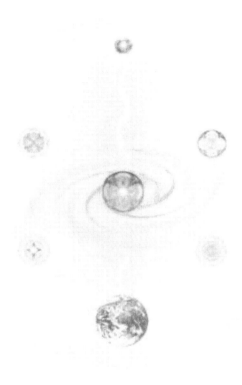

Vortex of Ennergy

The Vortex of Energy Meditation is an active meditation, which releases stress and toxins from the emotional, psychological, physical and energetic levels. This practice assists in the clarification and balance of the Five Fundamental Elements: Earth, Water, Fire, Air and Ether, the Seven Frequencies and the strengthening of the electromagnetic field. (Reference: This book)

Cycle of Energy

The Cycle of Energy through the Elements is a holistic approach that goes through the Five Elements and supports the process of manifesting an inspiration. The stages of this cycle represent a comprehensive process that includes the necessary resources and values, healthy relationships, a space of motivation, inspiration and clear thinking. This process provides the necessary holistic clarification to make conscious decisions. (Reference: Book "Elements on the Journey")

These three pathways complement each other like pieces of a puzzle. They support your development in your daily life. This provides accessible tools to advance on the path of life with harmony, compassion, and fullness.

~ Chapter 1 ~

THE DHARMI VORTEX OF ENERGY MEDITATION

This active Meditation facilitates the balance and the strengthening of the Five Elements and the Seven Frequencies (more detailed explanations upcoming). This practice supports your well-being and strengthens your vital energy and confidence. It helps you find balance and fluidity in your life, taking into account your deep inspirations and your external commitments and responsibilities. It is this search for harmony that guided and inspired me during the creation of this Meditation.

This active Meditation incorporates the pillars of our well-being and our personal development such as the magnetic field, mindfulness, heartfulness, chakras, visualization, Qigong, shamanism, the principles of sacred geometry, the dantiens and the bandhas. This active Meditation can also align your intention, your thoughts, your actions, and your relationships. This practice is simple, powerful and harmonious. It can take between 20 minutes and 1.5 hours, depending on your needs and the amount of time that you can devote to it.

Sometimes we deal with conflict between the voice of reason and the voice of the heart. We also feel a duality between the need to face our responsibilities, and the desire to pursue our dreams. Our own judgment of our emotions and our feelings can be the source of stress. In certain circumstances, we act too quickly and forget to take into consideration all the factors that affect our well-being. It is possible that your responsibility is to realize your dreams and manifest your life purpose.

When I was a child my mother would tell me that it would never work if people could have everything they wanted. Yet, I always disagreed with that statement. I believe that if everyone could tune into their heart and get what they want there would be peace and abundance for everyone. Of course, when the desire comes from greed, fear, attachment or an unhealthy ego then yes, her statement would make sense. Though, I prefer to look at life from the positive perspective thinking that people can tune into their hearts, and listen with love, compassion and gratitude.

This Meditation reconciles dualities and guides us towards a balance between different voices. According to the intent and the priority of the moment, it is possible to choose to perform The Vortex of Energy Meditation focusing on one of these four forms: clarification/ purification, alignment with an intention, extension and growth, and integration. During the process of clarification of thoughts and detachment, some people are able to make clear decisions without being drained by anxiety. They feel deep relaxation and increased energy. By practicing a regular meditation, others observe physical relief and healing of chronic diseases, (cystitis, back pain and headaches to mention a few). Others gain the courage to finish the projects they once put aside. In fact, most of them have realized that letting go fosters the manifestation of solutions in their lives. Indeed, Active Meditation can remove the ego and open a space for compassion, while honoring their own truths, beliefs and values.

The Path to Harmony: The components of the Vortex of Energy Meditation

The purification of the energy field is designed to strengthen your vitality and support the radiance of your innermost being. This Active Meditation practice releases stress and amplifies the magnetic field, leading you to wellness and a blissful feeling. To channel and activate the vital Qi energy, you must define the object of this Meditation. It is this predefined intention that will guide the exercise and allow for an enriching experience fostering growth.

This Active Meditation is based on carrying out precise movements accompanied by deep breaths and directed visualizations. This offers new opportunities beyond the linear system of thought.

When we feel distant from the state we desire, we often go looking outside ourselves. It is this distance, generated by our negative ego, that is the source of the stress that we feel which devours our vital energy. However, our positive ego, where we listen to our needs, is a helpful tool for us. Practicing this Meditation strengthens the magnetic field to attract what is necessary to create a change in our circumstances. Self confidence is bolstered through connection with the innermost being; when our intention, through use of the Meditation, is focused.

We are the creators of our perspective and are accountable for our actions. We can channel our emotions and direct our thoughts with creativity and positive intention. We become more receptive and selective, able to face the 1,001 little signs and choices that appear along our way.

The Vortex of Energy Meditation strengthens our capacity for concentration and sharpens the senses. This practice makes us much more spontaneous and open to the incidental events of everyday life. The attention we pay to our own inspirations, forces us to live in the moment, where we are focused on our purpose and resonance, and are attentive to our intentions. Such attention helps us improve our relationship with our surroundings. To do this, we must listen to our inner voice; the one that whispers very quietly and is often drowned out by our noisy ego.

You will benefit from this active meditation if:

You are a therapist or if you are in contact with many people. You can purify your energy space from outside influences that have affected you during the day. You will be mindful of the reality of constant giving and receiving, and you will develop a healthy balance.

You live in an environment where many electrical vibrations are present, (like those found in Wi-Fi networks or even radiation in the area where you live). You will strengthen your electromagnetic field and be better able to withstand some of those pressures and external radiation.

You tend to act in contradiction with your needs or your personal values. You can refocus and direct your actions in accordance with a specific intent.

You are looking for a match between your aspirations, your actions, and your interactions with your loved ones. This Meditation will help you reconsider your approach and clarify these connections.

You wish to better manage your stress and increase your energy. You will succeed in achieving this by using this Meditation regularly.

The Methodology of the Dharmi Vortex of Energy Meditation

This active Meditation aims to focus and clarify our point of reference, both in our personal relationships as well as in our professional, social, cultural and spiritual relationships. When we are more focused and aware, it is much easier to cope with the different life transitions and to accept constant change. By cleansing our minds, we can safely engage in every stage of our life.

Giuliano Geronymo. Facilitator of the Vortex of Energy Meditation and DHARMI - YOGA® teacher (RYT-200), shares his own view of the practice of the Vortex of Energy. When asked what key aspects he learned through this practice during training as a DHARMI Facilitator, he responded:

"The Vortex of Energy is one of the three basic pathways of the DHARMI Method. It can take place in a clockwise direction to purify the energy field and clean up any stress. In a counter clockwise direction, this Meditation improves alignment and balance and strengthens the vital energy. There is also another practice, which is carried out in a counterclockwise direction, used to solidify and strengthen an intention and our personal vibration. I have learned to use them when I need to come back «home» to a space of tranquility and harmony with my own essence, my own reality. This level of consciousness has allowed me to make decisions and to focus and clarify specific aspects of my life."

When asked how this Method has supported his evolution, Geronymo answered:

"This Meditation connects me with a purpose and intention beyond my negative ego. I have also learned to anchor myself more firmly in my human experience, and to accept certain physical or temporal aspects that I tended to resist. This Meditation helped me to untie knots of frustration. I now have more space for my reactions to life and everyday situations that I must face.

As a facilitator, guiding people through active Meditation, it's a very rewarding experience. People have been very receptive. I realized that my students, who were from different social backgrounds with very different paths, have all benefited from their first experience with this active Meditation. This Meditation is accessible to anyone of any age, from 9 to 90, because it adapts to everyone's state of mind. The more I guide people through the Map, the more I am inspired to continue to share and teach. I want to support the community and society in a process of welfare and evolution.»

An Active Meditation

I (Christelle Chopard), considered combining passive meditation, when the person's body is in a still position, with Active Meditation, when the physical body is in movement. The integration of the two supports the balance of Yin and Yang energy through the practice. Every step of the Meditation is guided by a specific intention, and offers movements on which to focus when the mind becomes distracted. Changes in concentration cause a slowdown, or an acceleration of the movement. When you notice that you stop or rush through the movement, you are reminded to return to the present moment with intention and clarity.

Movements activate the vital energy, and raise awareness of stress and resistance, affording a way for you to cleanse your body and mind from toxins and find more balance. This release passes through the assimilation of resources of energy, adding to your well-being and evoking the Five Bodies: physical, emotional, energetic, psychological and spiritual. This allows you to recognize the tensions that are present and to do something about it. You will therefore have the opportunity to observe your way of thinking and your reality of the moment. Sometimes you may feel the longrepressed emotions that resurface to be released and treated. It may happen that you feel resistance when performing one of the movements. In this case, the activation of Qi with precise intention will help you relieve any stress, anxieties and attachments. This resistance may also be linked to the memory of pain that no longer exists. It is stored in the emotional body, but is no longer in the current reality of the physical body. It is this memory of pain that we block that determines the magnitude of our actions. The concentration of thoughts, that you may encounter when using a mantra, can trigger a flood of emotions. Mantras (prayers in Sanskrit) guide your being to a vibrational alignment with the continuously repeated prayers. It is a very rewarding exercise in many styles of meditation.

This practice brings a mindful resonance to your whole being, aligning the Seven Frequencies with your intention. In this Meditation, we join focus with intention to control the thoughts that arise in our minds. To face your own past, by increasing compassion, brings an opportunity to develop new paradigms. Our human experience immerses us in a constant learning process. Each stage of our lives, and the different experiences that we encounter, present so many possibilities, awakening us to new potential, new skills and still unexplored perspectives.

Acceptance has a transformative power.

It is when we accept that, that we create space for the nature of change and transition to happen.

Sometimes, by the time we have reached a point where we finally understand something that has happened to us, it is already time to go onto the next thing. If you are a parent, you observe your child walking after many falls. As soon as he manages to walk, he or she is already eager to run, then ride a tricycle, then ski, then swim. Never stopping, never slowing, a child is always in forward motion. As a teenager, they run even faster, mostly from our attempts at parental control and then, in the blink of an eye, your child is an adult, presenting you with grandchildren, and an opportunity for you to develop a new role in this new cycle.

Sometimes you may be tempted to go backwards and resist certain changes. Tracking the Map allows you to accept evolution and navigate transitions with awareness, acceptance and direction. If you notice resistance to change, this can be a sign of a blockage somewhere. If the change is too radical and you lose control, it is a sign that you need to refocus to better manage this transition. The experience you gain will bring you the wisdom and the desire to move forward.

A few questions to bring mindfulness on how to navigate life transitions include:

Where is your anchor point?

Air Element: *Where is your mind at present?*

Fire Element: *How do you direct your actions?*

Water Element: *What are your main values?*

Earth Element: *Is your body stable and aligned with your intention?*

A clear mind and harmonious breathing bring life force and vital energy, relieving stress and removing toxins. When you are present and alert, you enter an area called "sattvic" in the Sanskrit language. You are totally relaxed while remaining fully alert and awake. The body and mind work together.

There are two fundamental nervous systems in our body that are in direct connection; one comes from the brain (the central nervous system), and the other from the stomach, the gutbrain (the enteric nervous system). When you focus on the essentials, it balances both present aspects to find a healthy balance between the yin and the yang. These two brains are in direct relationship, like the chicken and the egg. One cannot exist without the other. Some people develop the mental and psychological aspect more strongly, while others have a highly developed emotional perception and intelligence. These two aspects complement each other in the same way as the elements of Air and Water. Our thoughts (Air) strongly influence our emotional molecules (Water), and vice versa.

~ Chapter 2 ~

THE DIRECTION OF THOUGHT AND ALIGNMENT OF ENERGY.

There is a correlation between graphology and alignment in the Vortex of Energy Meditation, for a Mindful Resonance. For example, there is a clear parallel between the meaning of the alignment of the letter 'i' in graphology with its point and alignment in the Vortex of Energy Meditation.

We regularly hear the expression, "dot the 'i'. It is an easy way to remember the order, to keep your head on your shoulders, to clarify your communication, your thoughts and your relationships. However, it is difficult to put into practice.

When I studied graphology at the University of Handwriting Analysis of California, I learned the different meanings of the letter 'i'. The way the letter is written, the placement of the trunk [also called the stem of the i] (which symbolizes the body), and the placement of the dot reveal a specific aspect of the personality of the writer. What you write comes from the conscious, while the way in which you write it comes from the subconscious.

The letter 'i' reflects the level of attention and concentration and reveals whether your mind is focused or distracted. When the dot is clear, clean and close to the body of the letter, it reveals a personality attentive to details. This person will have good skills for performing administrative, accounting or organizational tasks. They may also have a talent for classical music, dance, architecture or interior design.

Some people may be so busy paying attention to the dot on their neighbor's 'i', that they forget their own. It is directly related to the phrase «The grass is always greener on the other side". I sometimes hear this from people who compare themselves with others and think that their neighbor's life is better than theirs. It is certain that as long as we pay more attention to the neighbor's grass than to our own gardens, the neighbor's grass will indeed be more beautiful. We must accept responsibility for our own garden, perfecting its space and alignment.

The dot on the 'i', reveals the direction of the thoughts of the person who writes it, as well as their ego and the base of their character. In English, the 'i' is a form for identifying oneself. I recently met a woman who works in the fashion industry. She has her own company and must choose new stock for Miami retail stores. Through graphology, I noticed that her dots were positioned toward the front of the trunk of her 'i'. Such placement identifies her as visionary, therefore she is good at anticipating what will be fashionable for next season—a useful character trait in her profession. However, it is difficult for her to remain attentive to every detail. She must often delegate certain administrative and accounting tasks to individuals who have abused her trust in the past. Following these disappointments, she made progress in her evolution by following the steps of the Vortex of Energy Meditation. During the process, she realized that her handwriting had begun to change. The dots of her 'i's are still forward, but are much closer to the trunk of the letter. She is now able to more closely monitor the work that she delegates to her employees, while continuing to use her visionary skills.

The dot on the 'i' reflects a person's level of attention and state of mind and this also applies to the alignment of our bodies. If we have good posture, our head rests squarely on our shoulders, in alignment with our spine.

The Internal Clock/Pendulum

Imagine that you have an internal pendulum on a string. This pendulum serves as a point of reference for wise and thoughtful decisions. However, when the alignment fails, and we have no connection with our true center, we lose contact with our own leadership qualities. It is at this point that our decisions and our actions are based on expectations of external circumstances, rather than on our own choices.

You may be familiar with the story of the mule that follows the carrot suspended at the end of a stick. The mule continues walking, unaware that it is a journey without end. The carrots remain distant goals that can be far out of reach. What matters is the journey, moving forward with clear intention and healthy values. Focusing on the carrots contributes to strengthening and lengthening the stick of frustration. Focusing on the journey brings satisfaction and leads to accomplishment.

First Exercise

This exercise allows you to experience a first feeling of what one intends to create, align, and strengthen with the Vortex of Energy Meditation.

Experience the alignment of the points on the body. Position your head on your shoulders, directing your thoughts and aligning your mind with your heart and your body. A spirit aligned with the body strengthens vitality and selfconfidence. It feels stronger, more focused and more attentive to current situations.

Sit comfortably on a chair, with your feet firmly on the ground. Your knees should be above your heels, aligned with your hips at a 90 degree angle.

Lay your hands on your thighs and straighten your back. A slight curve in the lower back is natural for some people, depending on your anatomy. But make sure even your hips and pelvic floor are well supported and connected to your body.

Take a few minutes to observe the sensations you feel along your spine while you are enjoying a state of awakening. People who have scoliosis will find themselves in a different position to those not afflicted, but each person will experience different sensations based on their reality. The reality of each person is reflected in their alignment, their life, and their way of thinking and acting. The best way to ensure a healthy body and spirit, is to start with a space of acceptance.

First become aware of your breath and see if your head tends to lean forward, backward, or to one particular side. This can be difficult to feel. Mainly because our way of holding our head becomes second nature. In our lives, we create many habits unconsciously, day after day, trauma after trauma. These become a habit—not a good one, but a habit nonetheless. Just as our bodies and our minds become accustomed to the television screen's continuous images which bombard our nervous systems with constant images and sounds. This can sometimes cause a dependency. Some people can no longer fall asleep without a television on nearby. By use of this electronic crutch, they try to silence their thoughts, their desires and their personal needs.

I've worked in shelters for traumatized women. Some of them thought it was normal that their husbands beat them. They had always expected it, sometimes they had even been convinced of its inevitability by their mothers, who themselves were victims of abuse. For them, love was demonstrated by punches.

Once people become aware of their own beliefs—positive and negative—they can do the clearing form of Meditation to release stress that has accumulated over time and impacted their energy. This approach is similar to a cleansing food detox, but the process takes place at a holistic level.

Now back to the exercise in a seated position; keep your back straight, without support unless it is really necessary.

Please be aware of your breathing. Note if you are taking short, light, deep, or jerky breaths. Observe without judgment. When you are well synchronized with your breathing, you are going to invite a more harmonious and profound level of mindfulness and reflection. Do not try to force these, but remain consistent and patient.

Now that you are stabilized, and that your breathing is regular, pay attention to the position of your head. Is your head leaning towards the front or the back? Does it fall to the left, or the right shoulder?

To help you a little, I suggest you tilt your head forward, consciously, and then reposition it. Repeat the same on each side and to the rear, always passing by the midpoint between each direction.

To search for this central point, direct your attention to the top of your head and follow its alignment down through your neck and throat and along your spine towards your heart, your solar plexus, the space between the navel and spine, and the base of your pelvic floor.

Take a few minutes to observe the relationship between each point and align them. When you inhale, you can direct the energy from your base, along your body, to the top of your head to uplift your energy. When you exhale, you can direct the energy from the sky to the Earth during this alignment to welcome vital energy, and surrender to the light and your intention. Repeat this breath and this visualization seven times.

Observe. Have you met resistance in your inner self? Sometimes the simplest exercise can be difficult to achieve. It takes a lot of attention, focus and clarity.

Equestrians learn early on the importance of anchoring and alignment. When you turn your head, and allow the message to pass through your spine towards the horse's spine very subtly or clearly, the animal will respond immediately, like a signal. The horse is responding to the movements of your head, even more than the movement of your hands, arms or feet. Your seat is placed directly on the horse's spine, the trunk of the 'i'. The spine is the center of attachment and bonding with its nervous system. The rider can have a very clear idea of their destination, but if they do not guide the horse properly, that destination will never be reached.

When you become more attentive to the positioning of the dot on the 'i', you can use it as an inner pendulum, a barometer inside yourself during the day. This sense of perception and alignment will allow you to make choices based on a new foundation and good clear intentions. Once you're familiar with this center point, which corresponds to the alignment between the third eye (the point, mind) and spine (sushumna, trunk, body), I invite you to explore further.

Think about the decisions you make today. Start with clear and simple things: What foods are you going to cook tonight? What movie are you going to watch? Then branch out into more difficult choices like about a conversation you wish to have with someone. Is it the right time to broach the subject, or is it better to wait?

Write a question on a sheet of paper with a few options of answers.

For example, *"Should I discuss my request for a vacation with my boss today?"*

List your options. For example:

1. It is better to wait and do it after I complete my report on Thursday.

2. I will ask him today no matter what.

3. We are too understaffed. I will wait until we hire a few more people, and then try to schedule the vacation.

Then, sit back and begin the alignment of the dot of the 'i' as translated into your body posture as described earlier. When you feel a clear alignment, raise the issues and options, one after the other. Take time to observe the response of your internal clock. Are you experiencing a feeling of strength and well-being, or anxiety and dread?

Taking a few minutes to focus, brings clarity and well-being during the day.

Centering Alignment Within, and Towards Your Environment.

Many traditions and religions use the symbolism of following the star that guides our steps. Imagine that star resides between our navel and spine. This focal point allows us to connect vital points within ourselves and to live with integrity.

We use the word "star" for celebrities who inspire us, and "shining star" for people who inspire the community. Everyone wants to follow the star or become one. We are bombarded by the notion of stars in advertisements, on television, in the movies and in all types of marketing. We can choose a star who inspires us and follow this source of inspiration, step-by-step. If we choose well, this can bring us closer us to our own star, the one that is within us, and which guides our steps on our own path of personal, professional, social, cultural and spiritual development.

Yet, the main purpose is to access and accept our own star within us. The star is our reason for living, an inspiration that lies beyond our primary desires of survival. We can choose to dance at our own pace and at the rhythm of the drum that unites us all. This space of acceptance opens us up to wisdom, compassion, leadership and trust.

The sky is full of stars. There are as many stars as there are directions, routes, paths and thoughts. Which is yours? It is possible that each of them leads to Rome? Were you born under a lucky star? We are all born under a star. They are all different, while being connected. Our responsibility is not to compare or judge them, but to do our best to live from positive intention.

~ Chapter 3 ~

INCORPORATING THE NATURAL LAWS, SEASONS, AND LUNAR CYCLES

The Lunar Cycle and the Personal Cycle.

Women are very sensitive to their 28 day moon cycle. Men are also affected by this cycle in their relationship with the women in their lives, the cycles of nature, and via their own feminine energy, since each of us has both a (female) yin and a (male) yang.

In the Vortex of Energy Meditation, this 28 day cycle goes through four stages of 7 days, each leading the evolution in harmony. In one way or another, we are all sensitive to the influence of the moon. Even if this is only by looking at its light in the night when it is full, or when it disappears behind some clouds before reappearing. Sometimes, the orb is so slight, we can only see a sliver. The moon appears most mysterious during an eclipse. Its cycles also affect tides and other natural events, setting the perfect stage for dynamic organic farming.

Are you too absorbed in your work, or do you have your eyes too glued to the computer screen or TV screen to even notice the moon's presence, and the rhythms of the seasons and nature?

In the early 1990s, I started a long journey around our planet at a time when there was no internet, no laptops, and no smartphones. I had a short trip of three to six months in Asia in mind when I began. But once I started, my exploration around the world grew longer and longer. I spent several weeks without being able to find a phone, or having any contact with my family. When a telephone could be found, connections were very bad and the conversations were often interrupted. I sometimes spent several days without talking with anyone who understood any of the three languages that I mastered during my time there. To rectify the situation, I let myself be guided by my instincts and intention. I often sat at night watching the moon in the middle of the starry sky. It was a way of getting closer to members of my family, or other people who were important to me at the time. I knew that they were going to see the same moon a few hours later and that thought comforted me.

The moon was for me a familiar reference point in a civilization and a culture so different from what I had known until then. I found a lot of solace immersing myself in this contemplation of the moon. I imagined conversations with it. I was using it to connect with my loved ones. Even when I was in reverie, these moments of sharing with my farflung loved ones allowed me to continue my travels, and to stay sane and not too lonely.

Now, there is Wi-Fi almost everywhere. We pass people walking all alone speaking loudly in the street. They react to things we cannot hear, laugh out loud, and even make grand gestures because of a conversation they are holding with someone on the other end of the line. I sometimes wonder what kind of conversation is more illusory? The imaginary conversation with the moon, or the one in which everyone speaks to a tiny microphone, sometimes forgetting to establish a genuine face to face conversation with another human being, sometimes not even hearing who, and if someone else is on the other side of the line. It becomes just a rote exercise.

I now live in the city, a place where everything is easily accessible. With a simple click on my computer, I often communicate with people on the other side of the world. But what I discovered during these cycles of sharing with nature still continues to carry me, and supports my balance in my everyday life. This connection with nature helps me stay receptive to sharing beyond distances. By remaining attentive to the natural cycles, I am able to maintain a harmonious life balance, and direct my actions with intent.

The Direct Relationship Between the Four Stages of the Vortex of Energy Meditation and the Lunar Cycles.

The first step of purification and clarification is related to the transition from the waning moon.

The second stage is that of renewal and rebirth, and is reflected in the new moon with the centering of vital energy space.

The third stage takes the form of expansion and solidification manifested during the waxing moon.

The fourth step is the space of integration and growth experienced with the full moon that gives us the opportunity to carry out a complete cycle. This helps us to focus and to move in harmony with universal laws and nature's cycles, towards a new reference point.

Is There a Better Model Than Nature Itself Where We Can Learn the Concept of Evolution?

As a child, I learned to listen and receive responses from nature. I always had the impression that the universe answered my questions by putting signs along my way. I interpret the language of nature such as the shape of clouds, a gust of wind, or a flower that falls on my shoulder. Sometimes I see a dragonfly in the city when I am asking for a sign about which direction to go. When I was lost at the end of my twoweek journey walking through Ladakh, in northern India, a goat appeared to guide my way to a village.

These small signs on our route can be very subtle and symbolic. Of course, there are also other signs that we must respect, such as the signs on the road and streets, the rules we should pay attention to when we live in a civilized society. There are also inspirations and other signs as we note the writing on a billboard, a quote in a book, or a message in the newspaper. However, it is important to be selective and know how to recognize the signs that support our way, as well as those that distract us and others that are tests to reaffirm our own values and truth. A clear intention, the awakening of our sensitivity, our sense of perception, and own alignment are all called into play to recognize these different signs.

Which Direction Corresponds to Which Element?

I have explored so many possibilities and find truth in all of them. In the Vortex of Energy Meditation, I chose to focus on one option that is comprehensive, simple, concise and practical in our daily lives.

It is a simple path, yet one that is not easy to pursue. Sometimes, it feels so natural, that it gives the feeling of "being too good to be true." Many people have made this remark through their experience of some of the steps in the Method, and in practicing the Meditation.

Most people think that we learn better from our mistakes. I consider that we learn more from what really works while programming ourselves, our response mechanisms in a way that is beneficial. We can focus on the problems and obstacles, or focus our attention towards possibilities. If someone cannot walk properly, are you going to learn from them? Or will you choose to learn from someone who walks with grace, strength and confidence?

The learning process requires a detachment from what is not suitable anymore, to focus on the righteous path. The journey from karma to dharma involves letting go of attachments to continue the journey with wisdom and intention. When we repeatedly make a mistake we become trained in that muscle memory and those core beliefs. Repeating a mistake repeatedly reinforces that path and affirmation. Sometimes it is best to pause and reflect before moving on in another direction.

My experience working with people, supporting their well-being and evolution, has shown that, in many cases, people feel comfortable in unhealthy lifestyle and relationships. When we succeed, and find a space of clarity and abundance, we get used to succeeding and following that path. When I chose the word DHARMI, my main intention was to lead people to follow a journey of ease and mindfulness the Dharmic path, in Dharma truthfulness and righteousness.

I notice that it is good to learn from what works, to bring attention to what is nurturing, healthy and uplifting. We acknowledge and recognize the shadow, yet our attention is mainly directed towards the light. Many shamanic traditions teach their tribe to focus more attention on positive behaviors. They emphasize positive attention, rather than negative attention. However, in many Western families, the children that cause the most trouble and drama are the ones that receive the most attention. The child who is doing well may feel punished for being so reliable, independent and kind.

When I learned about some traditions and the way they integrated the directions, I noticed that many of them include animals, colors and symbols to represent each direction. In certain Native American traditions, the North is the Air (white), the East is the Earth (red), the South is the Fire (yellow), and the West is the Water (black). However, some other traditions relate with the directions another way, with other colors related to each Element. For example, in Native American tradition, the Earth Element is represented by the color red. Yet, in the Kalachakra of the Tibetan mandala in Buddhist tradition, the Earth Element is represented by the color yellow. Both are right, in their own perspective.

In 1995, I undertook a long walk crossing the desert (the Naked Mountains) in Laddakh, an area that touches the Tibetan lands in the Himalayas. The yellow color of the eternal desert was quite overwhelming. When I couldn't find much food or water, I met a tribe of nomads on the way and they shared their butter yack tea and tsampa with me. I felt so grounded in this yellow atmosphere.

In 2003, when I spent some time in a tipi in a valley close to Sedona, Arizona in the United States, the canyons were reflecting different tones of red. Being in the valley, doing some trekking in the four mountains surrounding the camp, I could feel a deep connection to the land and Earth of the Native Americans. For me, the Red Rocks symbolized a strong sensation of the Earth Element in a red color.

I would suggest you explore different ways and observe what works best for you. Whether you choose a color, or no color, in the representation of the Elements, it will be fine for the realization of the Vortex of Energy Meditation for a Mindful Resonance. Though, if you choose to relate with a specific color for each specific Element, I recommend you stay in that perspective for a minimum of three months.

To keep it simple: I don't apply a color for each direction/ Element. I prefer to set a clear intention and observe its reflection in each one of them. If you need support in this quest, you can always contact us. What matters is that you take into consideration the Five Elements and the Seven Frequencies in all the processes of meditation, visualization and manifestation.

For an integral alignment, I take into consideration the seasons and location where you are to position the Elements. The Five Elements are: Earth, Water, Fire, Air and Ether.

The Seven Frequencies and positions are: Above-Spirit, Below-DNA-Ancestral, Within-Essence, The Four Cardinal Points - Mind (Air), Personality (Fire), Emotions (Water), and Physical (Earth).

In the northern hemisphere moving clockwise:
Winter, Earth, East
Spring, Water, East
Summer, Fire, East
Fall, Air, East

The directions of the Elements in the cardinal points have a direct relationship with the season. The predominant Element of the season is placed in the direction of the sunrise, the East.

Four cardinal points and four Elements plus above, below and within that form the seven frequencies. In the southern hemisphere, the main direction is the same, yet the positions of the cardinal points are moving counterclockwise. These specific movements and directions are related and aligned with the natural movements of the cycles and currents on the planet.

When a DHARMI Practitioner leads their client through a process of self or professional development, he or she always places the orientation of the answers in alignment with the Elements and corresponding direction. It is not the north in front of you; the north is true North, like a compass. This process and alignment support a more efficient alignment and clear process for the client's guidance and evolution.

When I give a private online consultation to a client in New York City, if they are facing the north and I am in front of my screen, I cannot be placed in a position that is not organic with theirs. I will face the South so I am still in front of them in relationship with the natural alignments. This way I can provide clear support while taking into consideration our alignment with integrity.

Is There a Better Model Than Nature and the Universe Itself for us to Learn the Concept of Evolution?

Nature teaches us and offers us lessons continuously. To me, life is a university that teaches us the awakening of wisdom through experiences, messages and signs on our way. I consider that the Universe brings us lessons that we can learn and grow from like getting a Master's degree at "Universeity".

I used to retreat to my grandmother's side when I felt unsafe. She told me stories from her own childhood and confided in me while we shared tea. She prepared the tea with the leftovers from her fruit tart; apple peels and cores and cherry pits. She added a few mint leaves and flowers that she had collected during her daily walk in the countryside. I reiterated in this part of the book's introduction, the story of the day when she received a message in the clouds regarding the end of the war and the new boundaries that would be set.

She taught me that each person receives their own messages in their own proper time. I learned to be patient. Thanks to my grandmother, I realized that everyone has their own way, even though we may live in the same family, in the same village, on the same land and surely under the same sky. Each of us is so different, while being so close to one another.

Being One leads us to a sense of Oneness.

At that time, my country village, my family and my friends were the entire universe to me. The sky and stars inspired me, but my perception of space was still limited. The vegetables came from my garden, the eggs came from hens we had, the milk came from cows of the peasant who lived a few minutes from my house. All my basic needs were covered in my small and great universe.

The creation of the Map (Method) is very symbolic for me because it reminds me of my grandmother's wisdom and the close relationship I developed with nature that surrounded me during my childhood, thanks to my family situation.

Each thing has its own rhythm. Each person has their own way while being united with others in a unique form. With experience, I realize that there are no possible shortcuts in our evolution. Each step on our Journey has its purpose and place in our life. When we accept our uniqueness, we have a better sense of union. We are at the right time, in the right place with the right people. Everything is in continuous movement, the hours, the days, the environment, the climate, the right place and the right time are constantly changing. The purpose of personal development is not to seek, to attach, or to separate, but to open to the present with more subtlety, to awaken our senses, to live with integrity, mind and heartfullness.

The Maps invite you to explore never traveled horizons, gaining your own perception and perspective on life. This exploration helps us make our choices with more clarity, opens us up to our inner pendulum, and helps us pursue a vision that reflects our essence and intention. The Vortex of Energy Meditation and the DHARMI Method respect the reality and pace of each person who practices them. Following the Maps helps you to clarify your way towards balance and clear alignment with your intention. While meditating, you acknowledge your own pace, yet you get closer to your truth with every step.

If you are reading these lines, it is a sign that you've embarked upon a personal quest and are open to new perspectives. I hope that everyone finds clarity, abundance and happiness by including these experiences in a personal way.

The Vortex of Energy Meditation is a dialogue and process of harmonization between the Five Elements, the Five Voices and the Seven Frequencies. The Five Voices are the voice of the mind, the voice of the heart, the voice of the body/needs, the voice of intuition, and the voice of the divine.

There are different ways to understand this dialogue. I think that each interpretation has a share of truth. In this book, I share with you my own interpretation and how I incorporated each of these Elements into the Vortex of Energy [DHARMI® Method]. Each Element is an energy, a voice and a tone; a frequency. How much of each is experienced differently depends on the stage of meditation, and how it falls into the context of the life of the person who is practicing it.

The holistic approach to the Five Elements allows us to construct a small ecosystem, with ourselves as a planet, in which all the Elements move under the influence of our surroundings, our environment and our emotions. As long as we are alive, these Five Elements are continuously in motion.

I have felt the force of nature's teachings. During my adolescence, when I felt uncertain, I went into the forest and I stood on a freshly cut tree trunk. In the middle of the forest, I tried to feel calm, stable and rooted like a tree. My first experience was so positive, I turned it into a ritual that I made use of during any difficult time in my life. This practice brought me a sense of support and a strong foundation under my feet that I didn't have in my life. It has helped me to make decisions, to build up confidence, and to find the strength to move on in very unsettling times.

Inspired by nature, Taoism teaches us key aspects of life, and sustains us to live in harmony and awareness. To be authentic with ourselves, we must accept our own nature. Our nature is made of elements, movements and relationships between our thoughts, emotions, desires and needs.

Some beliefs (Air Element) may limit our thoughts just as a sky covered with clouds limits our vision. It is a totally natural phenomenon. Unrestricted thoughts, instead, invite us to discover new horizons. They allow us to open our minds and our perspective.

We sometimes focus on unhealthy relationships that emotionally block us (Water Element). The same thing happens when a river is impeded by a large rock. The course of the flow remains blocked until the water pressure eventually clears the crossing. Paying attention to these movements helps us manage certain circumstances with awareness, acceptance and compassion.

Our experience of being human reminds us we must recognize perfection in imperfection; recognizing our feelings, our emotions and the way in which we live.

Some traditions take account of the ten frequencies: eight around us, one above us and one below us. The eight around us are a little similar to the Bagua in Feng Shui, in Chinese healing traditions. Also, some of the Native American traditions consider the eight directions around the medicine wheel.

Others paths take into account six frequencies: four around us, one above us and one below us. Some traditions speak of four (points/directions), others seven. Each perspective has its own truth in its approach.

Following many personal and professional experiences, I chose to consider seven frequencies based on the five main Elements in this active Meditation. The central axis is the Element Ether that includes the divine/above, the DNA/below, the heart center/source, intention. The four cardinal points are in interaction and continuous movement. They influence and support each other. They are the bridge between our central axis and the environment, surrounding us in this livingdimension. They are in direct communication with our environment and facilitate our interactions by supporting our communication and our relationships.

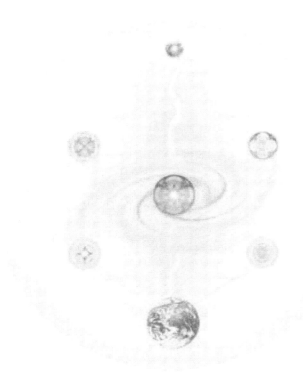

We can navigate from different levels of consciousness to awaken different perspectives in us and towards our life. Whatever happens, we always return to the center our source and our connection point the vital energy. Five fundamental Elements (Earth, Water, Fire, Air and Ether) are related, and between them allow the manifestation of our visions, our inspiration, our intentions and mainly our life purpose.

These forces can support a personal goal or higher inspiration. According to our commitment and our motives, we will direct these energies to serve healthy, pure, evolutionary intent or we will direct them to serve egocentric interests. These are the same forces, but used and oriented differently. I hope you'll turn your attention to positive intentions when you apply this knowledge and methodology in your life.

When the four Elements are distant from our true path, essence, values and central axis, it causes stress and a sense of separation from our Self. It is at this level that we focus our attention the most with the DHARMI Method: bridging our inner being, with our expressions, thoughts, actions, emotions towards our studies/cultural experiences, profession, hobbies, relationships and manifestations. If we manifest a lot, yet what we manifest (Earth) is not aligned with our well-being, mission and sense of self, we won't feel a sense of fulfillment, no matter how big the manifestation may be. Though, we must make sure we use a language, form or expression that is in tune with our environment and the society in which we live.

Each of these energy sources has different properties. We'll explore each Element as a fuel for the realization and expression of your dreams, and your intention. The Cycle of Energy (by the Five Elements), another pathway in the DHARMI Method, clearly guides you on the path that leads from inspiration to implementation, with integrity and healthy values. You will align the intention and focus of the Meditation with the Map through the Elements and viceversa for a holistic integral experience. (Reference: the book Elements on the Journey and the section Holistic Consultant Maps in the Manual).

~ Chapter 4 ~

THE VORTEX OF ENERGY MEDITATION IS A DIALOGUE AND HARMONIZATION PROCESS BETWEEN THE FIVE ELEMENTS, THE FOUR VOICES, AND THE SEVEN FRQUENCIES

Five Fundamental Elements

Earth, Water, Fire and Air are forms of embodiment and expression in our human body, and in the dimension in which we live during our years of earthly life. As mentioned above, each Element corresponds to a cardinal point. The Ether is the fifth Element that connects from the Center. This alignment passes through the vital energy and magnetism, and offers a feeling of unity, wholeness and harmony.

Each Element corresponds to a precise orientation, which varies according to the seasons. Thus, all facilitators and people who perform the Meditation and use the Map do so with the same orientation, by taking into consideration universal and planetary laws/rules.

 **Earth:** What vitality do you feel – how do you feel physically; do you feel healthy? This is the land that sustains and strengthens your immune system and activates the survival instinct. Contact with the Earth strengthens the physical body and the physical aspect. This Element is reflected in the bones, structure, discipline and organization. It is also directly related to the material aspect and prosperity; to the way you deal and organize your space, time and resources.

Water: How do you manage your relationships and your emotions? The connection with Water releases stress and reminds us to direct our energy towards healthy relationships. When we develop the potential of this Element, we learn to channel our emotions without judgment and with compassion, and intention. We take into consideration intuition, emotional capital and intelligence in this Element.

Fire: How do you direct your actions? What is your level of confidence and sense of leadership? The sun and the Fire increase energy, enthusiasm and motivation. This inner flame can burn us or burn others when we are not sure how to handle it. It is the main creation of our identity and ego; the personality with which we identify ourselves. Our feelings, self-confidence and self-esteem are wrapped up in this Element. It is in this Element with which we recognize our gifts and move towards our goals.

Air: Are your thought patterns and your beliefs limiting or clarifying? Breathing the fresh air leads you towards peace and clarity. This Element is mainly reflected in respiration, and represents the potential for reflection and the proper direction of our attention and level of concentration. We clarify our interest, relate with like-minded people, open our minds to new perspectives, and develop intelligence and cultural aspects in this Element.

Ether: Do you feel like there is an area of your life that is beyond logic or normal reasoning? The Element of Ether reminds you of the space of mystery, where luck or fate has its role and can direct your actions with respect and clarity, ensuring your evolution. The acceptance of this Element allows you to let go of the need to understand everything and follow your path with harmony, sometimes taking a leap of faith. This Element deserves special attention and can lead to a more supported development.

The field of Ether is reflected in the energy or vibrational level, making use of the wisdom and integrity of three main areas:

- Spiritual or universal

- Ancestral or DNA

- The essential source or heart center

The Ether Element connects all the other Elements and allows for the release of obstacles into an area of transcendence. The magnetic field recognizes these negative and positive vibrations. It is a major axis that you can access through the practice of meditation and Qigong. Ether is the way to connect to the source of creation. It reminds you about the mystery of life and your destiny, a space beyond your own personal power, which is also the source of that power.

When I guide couples who wish to become closer, I always remind them that there are three in the relationship, the two of them and a certain mystery, a certain fate, the essence of love. Awareness reminds us that we can do anything to the best of our ability, but that there are always certain aspects that are beyond our control.

Doctors are aware that although they make use of the newest technologies and do their very best using their education and skills, there is always room in their treatment of a patient for the mystery of fate. Fate sometimes brings fatality. We all die one day, despite the best efforts of doctors. It is part of the mystery of life. This aspect also reminds us of impermanence, revival, the birth of a child or a thought, and the start of a new day.

The Four Voices, which allow our expression and the creation of our life, are very complex. However, the search for simplicity can help us to connect the different inner voices to find a harmonious space of serenity. Sometimes we feel internal stress or that our Voices and needs are in conflict. Sometimes, we feel a great vacuum, when one of the Voices is extinguished or has been quelled or buried. What are these different Voices?

As a DHARMI Facilitator, we tune into the frequency of the four Voices to guide our clients:

Air: The Voice of our thoughts or sometimes the patterns of thoughts.

The Element of Air gives us the breath and the direction of our life. Our thoughts and our power of attention are specific. We have the opportunity to learn from experiences, studies and different cultures. We learn and draw conclusions from various parts of our brain. Our limbic system is directly linked to our emotional memory. Each area of our brain is linked to a specific aspect programmed to react, reflect or interpret. Our rational potential accessed by reflection (left hemisphere of our brain) and our potential for creativity and sensitivity (the right hemisphere) are in continuous relationship. Breathing and attention to the influence of each hemisphere allows us to keep a clear and healthy mind.

The tone of that voice comes from the breath and light and is reflective. You can practice it with the breath and lightness. Also, direct the communication in that dimension with clarity and breeze.

Fire: The Voice of our feelings, our motives and our desires.

The Element of Fire allows us to awaken the spark within us and a certain passion for life. Feelings as our inspirations are a characteristic of our human life. We develop a certain personality and image to identify and recognize ourselves. This Element primarily awakens during adolescence. It is during this stage that we embark on our search for self and discovery, that which illuminates our inner flame. This potential makes us both unique and unites us all.

The tone of that voice comes from the heart. When we guide clients approaching that Element/tonality we use the voice that comes from the thoracic cage area, lungs and a space of heartfulness. It is a full vibrant charismatic voice.

Water: The voice of our emotions, it is also the voice of our inner child, which can sometimes be very sensitive if there still open wounds. This Voice is linked to the enteric nervous system.

The Element of Water connects our feelings and supports our relationships. We all become emotional. We are sensitive, impressionable and feel the need to interact and have emotional ties to our surroundings. This quest for union forms a pleasant wellness and fluidity in our lives. The Element of Water gives us sensitivity, awakens our intuition and allows for the possibility of bringing harmony to our internal and external relationships.

The tone of that voice is emotional and sensitive. It is a tone that comes from your navel center from your stomach. It is usually contained and sensitive to invite and channel emotional expression.

Earth: The voice of our survival and our primal needs. The balance of our life is directly related to our discipline and the meeting of our physical and material needs.

The Element of the Earth allows prosperity, fertility, growth and creation to have the space needed to manifest. We learn to handle our vital survival needs. A good discipline, combined with family, food and material support bring us a sensation of well-being and good health. The Element of the Earth allows us to live well and organize our resources.

The tone of that voice is very grounded; it comes from the bones, from your foundation. It gives a sense of support, comfort and reliable space.

By undertaking the Vortex of Energy Meditation, we open the dialogue between these different Voices, and are looking for a point of understanding, alignment and balance between them. The Meditation adds vitality to each of these Voices. It is the Ether that unifies them, vitalizes them and allows their full operation.

At certain times, we go through moments during which it may seem difficult to access these Voices. You can practice through breath, sounds, visualization, introspection, or even mantras and prayers.

At that time, the transition to one of the other pathways in the Method supports a holistic developmental process. This process releases resistance, heals wounds from the past and balances the relationship between these Voices. It's like an internal committee that needs to meet regularly to establish a clear and balanced communication to find clarity and harmony. This space for reflection clarifies our position and takes into account our relationships with our surroundings, our family and our environment.

When the vibration and resonance are clearly aligned with intent, we live in a dimension that corresponds to it. It is possible to activate an intention and vibration to travel, called the "Quantum Energy Vibration" which I also call "Mindful Resonance".

~ 7 Frequencies~

Earth - form

Earth STRUCTURE is reflected in our physical, bodily, material and temporal space.

When you are in contact with the Earth (Pachamama, Gaia) you feel a beneficial support. Direct contact with the Earth deepens and strengthens this experience. The needs of the Earth are based on a discipline of healthy living through our diet, regular exercise and rest. It is also the area of prosperity.

The physical body is our Foundation and reminds us of our basic need to have a balanced life. From a holistic point of view, the Earth is connected to our resources, the management of survival instincts, and needs such as food, money, sexuality, basic aspects of hygiene, time and space.

Your connection and your relationship with this Element develop mainly during the last months of pregnancy and the first three years of your life. Babies learn slowly to take care of their own needs, learn to stand on their own feet, and learn the first resonance, tones and words to express their needs.

You are strongly influenced by your family and your traditions.

Taking care of your own needs; learning to stand on your own two feet with responsibility is one of the key aspects to develop the other Elements and grow with abundance. The deeper the roots, the higher you can fly.

The key to moving forward with confidence, freedom and security in your life is partially based on having a clear structure, organization, discipline, exercise and a healthy diet. Neither should you forget to manage your time and your money well.

The Earth Element also has a direct relationship with our sense of security and belonging. It is the Element that gives us the feeling of being enveloped and being part of something. A healthy relationship with one's family imparts confidence and a solid foundation. However, too strong a dependence on family or others outside oneself can block development at other levels.

The Earth needs air and space to be fertile and to enable growth. This Element needs a bit of each Element to be in balance. If you see nature, like in the Everglades [Florida, USA], where the land (the Earth) is swampy, almost only mangroves can grow in that area and animals that can survive in very wet unstable ground. If the Element of Water is too present in our natures, we are overly emotional and overly attached, which also restricts our growth. Not enough water is like the desert, and when our Earth is too dry, we ourselves may feel emotionally and physically exhausted. Sometimes, an excess of the Element of Fire appears in the Earth. The person can then be very distracted or hyperactive. This can also create a very unstable base.

The cycles of nature echo our own passages through various cycles in our lifetime. Excess or lack of an Element in our body signals a new stage in our existence. Like a flood, a wet season and a dry season are part of the cycles of nature. The daily practice of meditation promotes awareness of these changes. This helps manage and channel them to use them to their full advantage, with intention and mindfulness.

During the process, each participant restores and strengthens their connection with the energy and the natural strength of the Earth itself. In some specific cases, even a period of illness can be beneficial as that experience activates the immune system and strengthens the body. Approximately 85% of the ailments, illnesses or accidents that we experience through our lives are based on stress. As painful as they can be, they are also opportunities to learn something and release patterns, or change the rhythm or direction in our life. Sometimes they show us some level of stress and aspects in our life that have been put aside or ignored and are calling for attention. That is when we can combine Eastern and Western forms of healing, in which we combine mindfulness, heartfulness, inner work and external support to heal and move forward with a holistic approach.

I see the Winter as the season in strongest connection with the Earth. It is a time for calm, tranquility, assimilation and regeneration.

In connection with the lunar cycle, the new moon is the phase in which I see a space for rebirth where a new seed is planted to open new opportunities.

Mantra: I call on the strength of the Earth. I recognize the need for structure, discipline and a safe base in my life. I am establishing a healthy relationship with the physical, material and tangible aspect of myself. I respond to my needs to support my well-being and that of the people I encounter and the environment around me.

I appeal to the frequency of the Earth, which allows the manifestation at the physical and material realm. I am in harmony with the energy that allows the structure and organization in my life and with the foundation that provides the necessary resources for me to live in good health with integrity. I am listening to my needs and I respect the space of each. I take into account the physical and material field as I consider each sacred Element.

Purification: I'm listening to the physical symptoms that alert me along my way. I acknowledge the discomfort and blockages that influence me and open doors to new experiences. I will move through obstacles with mindfulness and open myself to the inner light and vital energy.

Expansion: I have channeled my intention so that it manifests itself physically. I have aligned my lifestyle to this intention. I am open to embody and experience it.

Inspiration: I have discipline and practice the ethics of healthy living. I organize my resources. I respect my space and with each space, the Earth Element brings fertility and prosperity. I call upon you with intention and respect the support and resources you offer, as well as the physical support, the vital energy and material needs you provide for our fulfillment. I take care of you as you take care of me. We are one.

Shamanic experiences:

I had the opportunity to participate in many rituals with various shamanic lineages in South America (where I lived for six years) Central and North America and Europe. I also had the chance to learn about aborigine cultures and rituals when I lived in Australia and experienced healing rituals and mantras from different traditions in Asia.

With Native American people, I practiced the ritual of the Temazcal, carried out in a sweat lodge, called an inipi. This ceremony is prepared with a clear intention and has many applications. Members of the tribe taught me that every step of the ritual is sacred.

A strategic location is chosen and a hut built with consciousness and intention. They then light the fire for the ceremony. The stones laid in the fire become hot and then, eventually red.

After smudging by sage, an invocation is made to the four cardinal points and each person enters the circular space within the sacred hut.

We then sit in a dark space, around the stones laid in the center. The redness of the stones evokes a return to the source in our mother's womb. The rhythms of the drums remind us of the beating of the heart. We experience its vibration together with the heat of the stones and release stress, attachments, and fear, breath after breath. We open ourselves up to the experience, release resistance and receive wisdom. It is a process of rebirth. This ritual gives us access to the deeper self.

A sacred ritual with the Element of the Earth is like a rebirth, moving and nurturing deeply within us. Taking into consideration the Element of the Earth reminds everyone of the need to create a harmonious, solid and sacred union space to allow conception, birth and receive a new being in our world. Parents prepare a house, a space for their future child. They balance their energy, clarify their intention and attune their frequency in order to prepare a calm space receptive to the new member of their family.

Water - Fluidity

Water – the fluidity, the current or water area is the space of emotional intelligence.

Water invites us to have healthy relationships and to channel our emotions with clarity, energy and intention. This item reminds us of our sensitivity, emotional values, and relationship with our inner child, as well as our relationship with our surroundings.

Water is directly related to our emotions, to the way we absorb life experiences and our inner child. I suggest you observe how you react to emotions. It is sometimes difficult to recognize our own emotions when they are very affected and influenced by those of the people around us.

What is browsing the emotional waves from a space of resistance, fluidity, compassion or stress?

Your connection with water, especially with the ocean, promotes the release of stress and opens the current on the path of life. Physically, water reflects the area of the stomach, the digestive system and the manifestation of the water throughout the body. Inflammation or the retention of liquids are signs of a reaction in the emotional body.

Water occurs in different forms: vapor, liquid, snow, clouds, and ice. This Element is flexible, adaptable and easily influenced, like us all.

Water reacts very quickly to its environment: temperature, winds, and movements. Our emotions are also in motion and permanent reaction, packaged and affected by our surroundings, but also by our own thoughts, decisions, movements, discipline, lifestyle and actions.

The correspondence between nature and our own actions: A rainy day reminds me to take my umbrella. A day where I'm particularly sensitive reminds me to be attentive and take handkerchiefs. A stormy day reminds me to be particularly alert as it may trigger emotional sensations or adrenaline. The calm always comes back after the storm. A profound relaxation comes after a wave of emotions. A tempered atmosphere give space and a healthy distance for clarification with peace.

If Water never moves it can become cloudy. When there is some movement, the Water circulates for purification and harmonious flow in relationships.

Water is directly related to the enteric nervous system [the gut brain]. Emotional memory instinctively responds to certain smells, colors and sounds. We create direct links with our experiences of the past. We are human beings, we are emotional, and we are just as much influenced as influencers.

When I speak of the inner child, I am referring to the voice that is linked to the emotional body, our sensitivity and our perception. Sometimes even after becoming adults, we keep very childish reactions. It happens that the emotions become so strong, deep and intense, they take over and we can lose all objectivity. It is a natural phenomenon that we can learn to manage when we become mindful of our emotional responses and sense of perception. Managing stress requires a lot of attention and energy. The repression of the emotions can be a great source of stress. It is important to allow the expression of our emotions and to channel them wisely. Emotions are like radars for intuition and require attention to be properly interpreted.

In a space of mindfulness and balance, the adult voice and objective can be attuned. We then take into account the voice of the intuition [inner child], without the need to be overwhelmed by our emotions. We can develop compassion and empathy and perhaps find that this enhances our relationship with others. We learn to listen to our feelings and our reactions. We learn to manage them better and discover our answers with more clarity.

Our adult voice often speaks to our sensitive voice like our parents spoke to us. When the relationship develops and improves, our adult voice develops parenting skills in alignment with our own intention and our values at this time in our life. Wisdom then awakens.

There are different levels to explore in our emotional universe. These are also the different levels to be taken into account in our relationships. With some friends, we can share some things that we won't be able to share with others.

There's an emotional intimacy that we reserve specifically for people with whom we have already developed a certain level of confidence. The sensitivity of this Element allows us to recognize the different levels in our relationships. (Reference: Elements on the Journey - Chapter on relationships and Elements in communication)

When taking into consideration the sensitivity of this Element, we can channel our emotions and manage our relationships with compassion and honesty. Sometimes we prefer to surf on the surface, while in other circumstances we dive right in.

Do you prefer to surf, channel, dive or fly?

How do you use your emotional intelligence?

Have you developed defense mechanisms that have the strength of a crocodile ready to attack and arise as soon as your inner child is affected? Have you drained your emotional body to ensure a stable income, to remain in a familiar, but harmful, space? Can you channel your emotions with wisdom and compassion?

Spring is the season in strongest connection with Water... a space in which to marshal our relationships and nurture our emotional body.

In connection with the lunar cycle, the crescent Moon is the phase in which I see the space for creation and growth to balance the Water Element.

Mantra: I appeal to the frequency of Water, which allows fluidity and makes me aware of my relationships and emotions. I become aware of my emotional memory and the ways in which those memories tie into my relationships. I choose to honor the space of my emotions. I let them appear and disappear without attachment or judgment. I acknowledge that my emotions are also my vital energy source. I am aware of the influence of my emotions on my decisions. I acknowledge the sensitivity that awakens creativity, intuition and my vital force. I develop the compassion that accompanies me in my relationships.

Purification: I accept my emotions and fears. I acknowledge their existence and greet them with gratitude, compassion and fluidity. I sail through my emotions. I dive into clear waters and nurture my emotional space.

Expansion: I channel my emotions with intention. It is reflected in my approach towards my relationships with transparency and fluidity.

I'm flexible and I adapt with gratitude to new perspectives.

Inspiration: Water, you are vulnerable and so strong, you can be transparent and fluid. You change and adapt with ease. I feel your presence and your movements continuously. I channel waves of emotions. You influence and are influenced. You relate and sometimes you spare me. You touch me. I take care of you. You take care of me. We are one.

Memories Evoked by the Water

I have swum in lakes and ponds, in pure water from a source. I have savored the tastes, intensities, the waves and the colors of the ocean in Florida, Australia, Jamaica and Peru, Spain's Cies Island and Israel. The Water in each location has specific characteristics.

Swimming in underground lakes has always inspired me. I have experienced this in Switzerland, Mexico and Jamaica. During my stay in Bolivia, I spent some time in the North of La Paz, in Sorata. A shaman told me of sacred ground with a subterranean lake. This place was full of legends and extraordinary stories that attracted my curiosity. It was dark in the cave, and the water was cool, but pleasant. I felt a call from the Earth, like a return to the source, and a need enfolded me and immersed me in the belly of my Mother, the Earth. Upon entering the water, in the complete dark, I had an impression of intense light, transparency and trust. This experience awakened certain subconscious memories and wounds related to my relationship with my Mother and my feminine source energy.

A few years later, I attended rituals with shamans in Mexico. I bathed in wonderful underground lakes known as Cenotes. Light filtered through in places and the turquoise reflections were almost surreal. My experience was totally different. I was overwhelmed by a sense of openness, lightness and freedom.

When I bathed in Lake Atitlan, a sacred lake in Guatemala, I heard voices. A language sounded and transmitted particular frequencies into my ears and body. Beyond the words, I have received a few key messages that I took into consideration during my stay in that beautiful country. These messages reminded me to respect the land and the ancestors. They also indicated that in this new period, the foreigner who goes there could also provide great support and resources. It thus contributed to supporting my well-being and allowed a certain balance in the development of the local community. Open and totally vulnerable, exposed to toxic influences and intrusion, the lake fell ill. Now, it needed support and resources to be able to regain its balance. Some people have taken the situation in hand to find a solution and to take care of this sacred space, this center of high energies and resources for the culture and community in the area.

Each person has a scale of trust and different needs. It depends on our personality, our history, our childhood and our state of mind at strategic times in our lives. If we really need to be saved, we will awaken the survival instinct that is bound to the Element of Earth. While if we are well, we can be more selective, posed and receptive to what truly suits us.

In the emotional aspect, I take into consideration healthy relationships and the potential to channel our emotions with clarity and intention. I do not think that there are negative emotions. It is our own perspective, our own judgments and our own actions that transform emotions into feeling positive or negative.

The awakening of anger reveals our emotional boundaries and the need to say no if necessary. If this force is repressed, it may be reflected by a lack of selfesteem and a loss of energy. If this force explodes and becomes uncontrollable, it can hurt. To be able to channel our emotions, we must first learn to listen to that inner voice, which is both sensitive, vulnerable and strong.

Our emotions are directly linked to our vital energy, in the strength of the Earth, survival, protection, manifestation and fertility.

When we are overwhelmed by our emotions, we easily lose energy. When I studied the Grinberg™ method in 1990, he taught us to be mindful of the emotional waves. We were able to detect the arrival and intensity of the emotion. Go to the top and channel: it is like surfing on a wave. We learned to pay attention to the sensations without getting carried away by them. When we recognize the culmination of emotion, we know where we stop. It is how we receive the strength and use the power of this energy.

We must practice regularly to learn how to handle the waves of emotions and strengthen ourselves. It's like learning to surf the waves. We start with small waves to gain confidence. After beginning with small ones, we explore bigger waves. It is not necessary to force and to push more. Life is already pretty traumatic as it is, without needing to add any more traumas. Yet, a space for play, a sense of purpose that comes from emotions that are triggered, and creativity in life are vital for us to stay uplifted and inspired.

Like the tides in the ocean, the ups and downs are part of the nature of Water and our overall balance. Trying to constantly remain at the same level can create more energy blockages and imbalances than if one accepts the natural movements by introducing flexibility and fluidity into our lives, our relationships and our evolution.

Fire - the dynamic and movement

Fire, its energy is reflected in movement, selfesteem, action or lack of direction. Fire evokes the feelings that are often caused by emotions. This frequency inspires enthusiasm and awakens motivation. Physically, Fire is reflected through the heart pulsation, movement and our muscles. By practicing the Meditation, you awaken and balance your inner flame with clarity and direction. Fire is also a space of expression and self-confidence. It is the identity that you create and with whom you choose to express yourself. Ask yourself how you direct your actions and if you have good selfesteem. Did you learn to receive attention in achieving positive actions for yourself and those around you? Did you have to carry out absurd acts to receive attention? Are you more focused on negative attention than on positive attention?

Meditation activates the Sun, and Fire grows energy, enthusiasm and motivation. This inner flame can sometimes burn us, or burn others when we are not clear on how to handle it.

The correspondences between nature and our own way of living:

When the sun rises, it reminds us of the need to wake up. Its light invites us to open our eyes. Its heat invites us to share. Suddenly, a cool breeze passes. It refreshes the environment and it is time for us to recover from the heat. An inspiration awakens our energy, and we become motivated. We want to express ourselves, to share with those around us, and then we're suddenly influenced by a cold judgment, which affects our energy level. This is when it's time to measure the intensity and direction of our actions, to maintain a healthy selfesteem, and to act with healthy values. A match ignites and lights a candle. After a very short and intense moment the match is extinct, while the candle shines harmoniously. It creates light in the darkness of night and sends us heat and clarity. The flame represents life, movement, dynamics, rhythm, and color. A project is inspired by a dream. This fleeting vision acts as a sign, awakening our inner Fire. The project can motivate a group of people. It can arouse them from their sleep, awakening positive energy, and creating a dynamic in a warm, pleasant rhythm and energy.

In the element of Fire, we give space to our inspirations. We go about our actions with confidence and warmth. Our actions are born of pure intention, without effort, but with a unique and consistent force. It is mainly in the frequency of Fire that we learn to measure our actions, our motivations, our feelings, and our ego. A healthy ego not only takes into consideration its personal firewall, but also the space of those around it. It establishes a balanced exchange. Sometimes the inner Fire can run hot, giving too much, and forgetting to take its own needs into consideration. Conversely, it can also be overloaded by an ego only focused on its personal well-being, without any consideration for other people. Throughout the years and our different experiences, we develop patterns of conduct that influence us in our behavior, our relationships, and our achievements. We tend to stay in our comfort zone.

In the DHARMI Method, Summer is the season that has a strong connection with Fire – it's a time of crops and development.

In connection with the lunar cycle, the full moon is the phase in which I see the space of fullness and abundance directly related to the Fire Element.

Mantra: I call upon the energy of Fire. I take into consideration my inspirations and feelings. I like the rising expression of my heart. I open to the possibility of reflecting my intentions in my actions and my behavior. I am sensitive to the people around me, and I look for a balance in my dance, my expression and my interactions. However, I am determined to accept responsibility for my actions with compassion and intention.

Purification: I accept my ego and I forgive the role I attached to myself. I thank this character, this great friend who has supported me in difficult situations. I release my attachments and open myself up to new possibilities.

Expansion: I express my intention in my actions. My intention is based on pure feelings that come from the heart and allow me to grow with confidence.

Inspiration:

Fire, you move and you revive. You can be warm, burning and sometimes crippling.

You encourage me. I feel your rhythm in my heart.

I act with intention.

You inspire me to dance at your pace.

You come closer and I use your energy to shine with positive intention.

I take care of you.

You take care of me.

We are one.

We have a body, complete with memories, emotions, muscle and brain. What happens when you say: "I understand and will stop doing it, yet continue to repeat the same behavior?"

first love relationships, passions, and desires. It is a stage of exploration, a search for identity and self-confidence.

The way we direct our actions, form of expression, behavior and movements is the concrete representation of this Element. Sometimes, we feel an inner conflict to act in a manner that does not correspond with our values or intentions. Sometimes we feel conflict between our desires and our values or expectations. It is a sensation that can resemble confrontation. There is a very fine line between struggle, resistance, and confrontation, and the determination and courage that enable development.

Fire represents feelings. Water is very emotionally sensitive. It is therefore in direct connection with Fire. Air observes and directs these aspects. It is therefore, our interpretation in direct relationship with how we perceive, judge, or direct our actions and respond to our emotions. Earth contains and allows for manifestation, channeling, or release.

Feelings cause us to act in a certain way. Romantic feelings arise in Fire and Water elements. They motivate, awaken and open our hearts. Fire balances the emotions between thoughts and communication, allowing for open expression, a feeling of sharing and unity.

Remember that a flame is always in motion. Movement is its nature. The speed of its dance varies according to the intensity of emotion, such as boredom at one end of the spectrum and passion at the other. Content, healthy directed movement allows for a sense of self. Self-confidence is reflected at various levels. Fire is the central Element of self-confidence. It is the point of union, the spark and the source of pure feeling. Fire gives us a sense of purpose, it represents our sense of identity, the role we take, and the personality we choose to have. It is the form of expression of our talents and motivations that uplifts our self-confidence, and gives us a sense of purpose and fulfillment.

Air - thoughts

Air represents the psychological domain, your thoughts, your potential for reflection and the direction of your attention. This space is directly related to the culture and beliefs that you have developed during your life experiences.

This Element supports clear reflection. What is your perception of life and the circumstances that you encounter? What judgments and thought patterns have you developed? Do they originate from a healthy space, devoid of judgment or the memory of trauma, fear, and disappointment? Do you have expectations that create some stress in your life? What are your thought patterns and beliefs that either limit you, or help you to see more clearly? Do you consider yourself intelligent? Do you have a good memory and have you developed critical thinking? What are your main interests? Breathing, fresh air, a space for reflection and meditation helps to move us towards peace and clarity. This area of concentration on thoughts helps direct them with intention. Thoughts need exercise as much as our physical body. It's like training a new muscle through intellectual stimulation.

The correlation between nature and our way of living

Watching the sky, I observe the clouds that pass. They move and change shape, color, tone and texture. They appear and disappear. They become heavy and a storm ensues. The wind blows and flushes them away. Rain moisturizes the Earth. The clouds form images and drawings like a language from the

universe. Suddenly the sky is clear with a bright sun, so ins-
piring – it is like moving art. I look at life and I observe my
thoughts, which carry judgments and reflections. They change
my perspective and outlook. When I become attached to out-
comes I   create stress and suffering. When I take a moment
of reflection, some deep breaths and I clarify my intention, it
helps to organize my thoughts, and instead opens me up to new
opportunities. Emotions surface, and tears may flow, yet they
soothe my heart and open my mind to new possibilities.

Positive thoughts and a clear perspective allow us to clarify our ideas, our interests and our values. Concentration, reflection, study, and meditation are key to exercising the mind
and maintaining balance. The same applies to the pysche as it
does to the physical body; we need to stay healthy in both. It
is important to implement physical and mental activity to avoid
injury. Redirecting our attention with the use of visualization,
helps to retrain neuropathways dedicated to supporting our well-
being and development. If we start the day with clarity and intention, we will be attentive to certain aspects and synchronicities, coincidences, and connections on our path. If our thoughts
are scattered, it will be difficult to move in a clear direction.

Our belief system tends to be based on internal and external expectations. We can choose to pursue our goals from
a place of clear intention, by respecting our values and taking
responsibility for our actions and decisions in the process.

The mind works like a parachute; it is efficient when it is
open, connected and well directed. The air is invisible, as are
our thoughts, but its influence is strong. When I fly my kite in
the air, I have to take into account the wind direction, speed and
gust, and my intention and the direction in which I would like to
go. The wind is invisible, which requires a high level of attention
and alertness to navigate the waves with confidence and grace
while kitesurfing.

Lama Dorje, a Tibetan Lama who works closely with the organization Condor Blanco, shared a message of great wisdom in an abundance ceremony that I attended, "Everything is perfect. The only imperfections come from our perception."

Personally, I see the Fall as a season in strong connection with the Air. It is a space for harvest and letting go or surrendering.

In connection with the lunar cycle, the waning Moon is the phase in which I see a space for cleaning, selection and clarification. It is a cycle closely related to the Air Element.

Mantra: I appeal to the Element of Air to bring clarity and lightness to my thoughts. I respect this Element. I acknowledge every breath and every thought. I become aware of the knowledge and wisdom that this Element brings to my life. I focus on my intention. I choose a path of clarity, reflection and intelligence. I release thought patterns that inhibit my concentration and my well-being. I observe with equanimity and compassion.

Purification: I accept and I forgive my beliefs and judgments that have been strengthened over my life. I open up to a new perspective with respect and freedom.

Expansion: I lead my thoughts with positive intent. I reflect. I express myself and communicate with clarity.

Inspiration:

Air

I observe you.

I clarify my thoughts.

I acknowledge my perspective.

You open my mind.

I discover new possibilities.

You inspire me.

You renew my space.

I breathe.

I hear you whispering.

I take care of you.

You take care of me.

We are one.

Breathing is the physical aspect that is linked directly to our thoughts. During the Meditation, concentrate on the Element of Air, by breathing and balancing the central nervous system. This tranquility will soothe not only your thoughts, but also your emotions and your whole metabolism. When our minds start to heat up and our thoughts run rampant, they are guided by our concerns and stress. We then lose our concentration and sight of our goals. When we are overwhelmed by emotions, it is the element of Water, that takes over and our mind becomes confused and doubtful.

Memory Evoked by the Element of Air

When I learned how to kite surf, I was very clumsy. I was often taken by wind gusts. In less than a second of inattention, I found myself on the beach on my stomach with my trainer kite wound around a palm tree, a few meters away. In fact, the wind surprised me as soon as my attention was distracted. It's as if it was reminding me to keep listening, to be alert in the present moment, and to be sensitive to the invisible.

I persisted, I focused, and I learned various styles of kite surfing, in various conditions, such as the different directions and intensities of the wind and waves on oceans, lakes, and beaches. I also learned different techniques and tricks. This was training for new muscles, both in my attention, my actions and muscle memory. Kite surfing is a good way to live in the present moment. We focus our attention, our actions and our movements, while taking into consideration the environment.

I see the wind as the Element of Air, the ocean the Element of Water, and we kite surfers as moving with grace like dancers combining different skills and Elements. Other ways of experiencing the Air Element are in learning new languages and discovering other perspectives and cultures. It opens the mind and develops different parts of our psyche. To keep a healthy mind, we need intellectual stimulation daily, in one way or another.

Ether Element

Ether creates a link between all the Elements and the three fundamental points that are the following frequencies: the voice of the heart, the universal consciousness, and our ancestors. In our heart, we find our true essence. But we are influenced by cosmic, universal movements, as well as our DNA, our ancestors, our education and the people who surround us.

take into consideration 3 Frequencies in this Element:

- The way of the heart

- The divine light – life source

- The lineage, inheritance from ancestors - DNA

 The way of the heart

The heart is our central station, the point of union and connection between all the colors of the rainbow.

By listening to the heart, we can recognize our true purpose as well as any imbalances, conflicts, desires and aspirations that require our attention. The moments of redistribution are essential for developing a balance. Take a few minutes daily to meditate and to listen and find balance. Meditation, mindfulness and perception arouse a particular harmonious connection. We can navigate through the various energy waves according to our intention. This intention and subtle space opens the door to a new reality.

I have often heard program participants declare: «If I position myself in this space of mindfulness, in this perspective in these situations, it will change my life,» and that is what happens. We may engage in certain directions from a space of love. There is no error when it comes from the heart. Being positioned in the heart at a central level, helps us to acquire more clarity towards life and its circumstances. Positioned in the center, we can find a healthy space and an authentic way of expression. Personal magnetism, also known as charisma, comes from this space.

Unconditional love (agape) comes from this central point, while other types of love come from the need for a sense of belonging, or are conditioned by certain beliefs and expectations.

They are sometimes related to the ego and require attention for a healthy self-esteem. We sometimes feel a sense of separation between the heart and the other frequencies. This can lead to depression, stress, or a feeling of lack. It is the conflict between one or another of the frequencies that causes internal stress. (Reference: Holistic approach to stress awareness and management in the book Elements on the Journey.)

Searching for harmony and the links between the different frequencies from the heart create a harmonious balance and a feeling of fullness and well-being. From there we can develop a harmony that is reflected in our overall balance. Sometimes we are tempted to leave this space out of love for another person. We may abandon our self-esteem by searching to be loved or to demonstrate our affection. Rather than bringing us closer, this may sometimes cause stress and distance. Love is in the essence and must radiate naturally. It shares purely and with compassion.

When we accept our own way and own role, we find peace within ourselves and those around us. Everyone has their own way and their own role, which they meet to create a sense of union. We want to live in harmony with our surroundings. Sometimes we give priority to our place in society, in the family, or in our environment that guides us towards an area of balance and abundance. This foundation will later allow development at other levels, unless the person loses their values and gets carried away by vanity and greed in the process.

Meditating regularly will help you to take a step back to refocus yourself. You can then return to your duties, your intention, your relationships and your projects with clarity, compassion and confidence.

The heart has a unique potential for charisma, interaction, motivation, leadership, love and compassion. It is a central and essential space.

Mantra: I appeal to my inner voice, the voice of the heart that directs my steps with wisdom. I trust my inner guide, which leads me to my reason to be. I advance with ease on my way and I honor my values with respect and a sense of purpose. I am alert, confident and compassionate. I direct my steps with intention, love and integrity.

Purification: I accept and I forgive conflicts and internal stresses. I acknowledge the duality that manifests and the tightness I can feel in my life. I recharge my batteries in love, compassion and peace.

Expansion: I open up to the vibration of my heart, my gifts and my essence. I welcome this expression in my whole being. The voice of the heart is pure and magnetic.

Inspiration:

The way of the heart.

I get wisdom.

I open my heart to love.

I radiate a pure and authentic intention.

You remind me to act with compassion.

I feel serenity and fullness.

You love unconditionally.

I accept who I am.

I project myself with confidence.

I take care of you.

You take care of me.

We are One.

Divine Guidance

The tone of our intention and our spiritual path - the beyond.

Beyond space corresponds to the universal consciousness, the mindfulness that gives us a sense of purpose. This frequency is beyond judgments, attachments and fears. It is a pure and authentic space of liberation in its shape, its color and its vibration. It is both connected and unique. It is the eye, the nothingness, and the all. Being aware of this divine energy and force helps us to manage our thoughts. This life, this divine source that comforts and gives us the strength and the trust that we need to move forward with love, inspiration and compassion. Memory and information present in the Air are a portal to endless opportunities.

I am referring to the Element of Ether to evoke the star under which we are born. Astrology and numerology facilitate understanding of certain influences that occur in our lifetime depending of the time, day and location we were born. We can take these influences into consideration with clarity in following a path into the light when we focus on a positive intention.

Some people call this light God, Buddha, Allah, Life Force, Prana, Qi, Vital Energy; everyone has their own beliefs and their own perception of this frequency within this space.

The Correlation between nature and our own ways of living.

Many people feel the influence of the full moon on their state of mind and emotions. The tide, the ocean and our natural environment reflect its influence.

At night, I look at the sky and I observe the stars. In the day, I look at the sky and I see the empty space. Far away on the horizon, there is a fine line where boats disappear. Far up in the sky, there is a dimension where aircraft also disappear. Yet everything continues to exist in another time and space. At night, I dream that anything is possible. During the day, I see only the tangible, a limited space. Somewhere deep in my thoughts, there is a line that separates my rational thoughts from others. Later in my dreams, there is a line where my conscious thoughts and my reasoning disappear. The existence is always present, filled with mysteries.

We are inspired to follow our dreams. This inspiration reveals new opportunities to achieve our destiny beyond our daily goals.

Mantra: I appeal to the essential source. I receive light from the beyond to release my whole being of stress and toxins. I channel the inspiration that comes from my inner voice and I open up to new perspectives.

Purification: I choose freedom. I entrust myself to the light and the divine essence that guides my steps.

Expansion: I am in harmony with my intention and I recognize the synchronicities that guide me on my way. I am alert and I equip myself with vital energy.

Inspiration:

Divine Source:

Intention, light, I have faith.

I open to the universal intelligence.

You bring messages on my journey.

I'm listening.

You whisper in your language.

You reveal to me my reason for living, guiding me step-by-step.

You remind me of the mystery of the beyond.

I take care of you.

You take care of me.

We are one.

 DNA

The frequency of our DNA programming comes from our ancestors. It is our heritage. It is the space of our roots, the family tree, and the lineage that we are part of.

When we connect with the Earth under our feet, we link to the roots and the core of our planet. We feel that it puts us in contact with all beings who are in touch with this earth at this time. This gives a sense of community, a sense of belonging, of mutual support and responsibility beyond our personal space. Our roots remind us that every step, every thought, and every action affects all human beings and the environment that surround us. This generates a new outlet of conscience for many people on topics such as ecology, the environment, and the recognition and respect of each space.

Whether you are born in a woman's or a man's body, whether your skin is white or colored, whether you're big or small, these foundations and footprints don't fully define you, yet they are big influences on who you are, the path you walk and your karmic definition. Some people experience conflict with the color of their skin, their size, their family, and the society in which they were born. Being at peace with oneself and one's reality and its ancestors is essential to be able to live in harmony. You can use your resources and perceive your origins as limits or opportunities in your life.

Memory Evoked by the Element of Ether

I participated in shamanic rituals with a wise Dutch shaman: *Jan Van der Stappen*. He invited us to visualize ourselves in a temple with all our ancestors. It is a way to be at peace and to deal with the programming that runs in our veins, in the memory of our DNA, without feeling like a victim, attached or fearful of our linage. Indeed, we are all influenced by our ancestors and the physical body, time, and space in which we live. However, we can choose to see it as a wall that stops us or a door that opens and allows us to fulfill our life's purpose.

We often experience an inner struggle and deep stress directly linked to our roots, our family and our culture. On the other hand, it is possible to change our perception; how we act and how we connect. This requires a process of reprogramming, a transition from karma (life experiences) to dharma (integration of the life experiences towards transcendence and wisdom). The purpose of this approach is to better manage our situation and quality of life. Directing our attention in a way that takes into consideration this reality, while also opening opportunities for evolution and the manifestation of your desires, purpose, talents and inspirations.

Mantra: I appeal to my source and my resources with respect and gratitude. I acknowledge my lineage, my ancestors and my heritage. I align my steps and actions with my intention. My footprint, my brand will affect all human beings and the vibration of our beautiful planet, with clarity and with the intention that I reflect.

Purification: I accept and forgive my ancestors and my lineage. I acknowledge the traditions and influences of my roots and my family tree. I care and I harmonize my roots with intention to clarify my base and my resources.

Expansion: I reinforce my roots with intention. I experience the vibration of each step to support my consciousness and well-being on Earth. I acknowledge my influence on people around me and my environment.

Inspiration:

My footprint and my inheritance.

You support and you influence me.

I would like to leave my mark.

I understand your programming and your direction.

You reflect my intention.

I respond with commitment.

You are my family tree.

I can remain attached.

I can grow and become a fruit to ripen.

I can let go and be reborn.

My lineage will always be.

I take care of you.

You take care of me.

We are one.

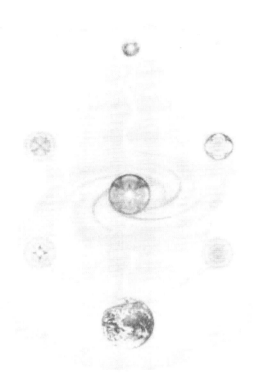

ENERGY,
THE MYSTERY AND THE SYNCRONICITIES

We will further explore this mystery that binds us all with each other, which I named Ether in the Meditation. We need to be aware that, while we are doing our best, some factors are beyond our control.

Some physicists have discovered that we live in a world made up mainly of space. This leads us to ask ourselves: is it matter that dominates space, or space that dominates matter? If there is more space than matter, what really matters?

Ether is reflected at a spiritual level, in wisdom and integrity. It is this Element that binds all the other Elements. This creates a space of transcendence and freedom of attachments. The magnetic field recognizes the difference between these negative and positive vibrations. This is an essential quality that you can access with the practice of meditation and activation of the vital energy [Pranayama and Qigong]. Ether is the way to connect with the source of creation, with the fuel of life. It reminds us of the area of mystery and destiny, something beyond our power which is also its very source.

This aspect also reminds us of impermanence and constant revivals: a sunrise, a new idea, and a new life. Being aware of this energy and divine force helps us to better manage our space, our thoughts and to be aware of the frequency and the way that inspires us.

With active meditation, mindfulness, and concentration, we can access this particular frequency. We can navigate through different energy waves and perspectives. It is a bit like choosing the radio program you want to listen to, but at a much subtler level. We draw our inspiration from rewarding aspects. We interpret what we see in different ways.

In 1993, a group of people met in Washington, D.C. to meditate together twice a day and observe the level of influence of electromagnetic frequency on the community. They found that violent crime decreased by 23.6% in the first four weeks alone. A frequency of peace, love, and light affects the community in a healthy way. When you meditate, you don't do it just for you. You also support the well-being of everyone around.

Establish an intention and you open a subtle space, the door to a new reality. Somehow the ether is the Qi (vital energy), prana and the quantum. Within this vibrational etheric dimension, it is matter of wave-length, the connection that one has, or does not have with people, perceptions or interests.

During my travels, I crossed different countries and cultures, and met many types of people. These encounters generated a connection with their vibration and their fundamental values, melding them into one. It is indeed strange that, all over the world, I have met people who like me were looking for evolution, and were in search of well-being, harmony, happiness and freedom. Some people unite based on their vibration of attraction and values. This aspect is directly inspired by our relationship with the four basic Elements (Earth/needs, Water/relations, Fire/motivations, Air/interest). When we release pressure and stress, we can access this vibrational level. This requires a certain letting go in order to leave place to faith, to trust beyond basic safety and instant gratification.

I was often surprised that what brought me serenity was not always the most comfortable, or one that would bring me certain guarantees of material and emotional well-being or security. Everybody has a different path and priorities. The DHARMI Method invites everyone to follow their own path with compassion and respect. This Meditation supports each person in finding their personal alignment and their own truth.

It is not me who knows better than you. I have my own knowledge and wisdom that I share with you. I invite you to awaken and to take into consideration your own wisdom, perspective and values. Each is complete, and influences, strengthens and supports itself to advance to a community level. When you follow a process of personal development with a DHARMI facilitator, you awaken a new potential that you can use at your own pace to access more clarity.

Ether is the Element that supports the connection between the mind and the body. Some traditions evoke two souls: the spiritual soul and the ancestral soul. The spiritual soul reflects our destiny, our source and our star. Some speak of past lives and memories that it carries. The ancestral soul is directly related to our DNA, our family legacy, lineage and family tree. I consider that there is a third one, the essence, vibration and resonance that allow union and compassion. It comes from the heart, the source for every healthy loving relationship with your family, yourself, and fellow human beings. It defines your true Self and uniqueness that connects you with all.

Death occurs when vital energy disconnects from the body. The four Elements (Earth, Water, Fire and Air) support expression and the process of reflection, our potential for action and events during our short life as a human being. One day, a person who regularly used the DHARMI Method in everyday life told me, «It's fascinating to be incarnated in this human experience. We can learn so much, discover, and use our senses. I am sincerely grateful to be a human being."

Many spiritual paths are concentrated on life's etheric level. Personally, I consider that the process of life on Earth (with all our emotions, thoughts, feelings and inspirations) forms a part of our learning process - our human experience. I think that basically we are all spiritual. It is our human experience, our way of life that differentiates us, and offers us tools for channeling and expressing our intentions and fulfilling our responsibilities. This reflects the spiritual aspect in daily life. It is sometimes really hard to channel our emotions, direct our thoughts, express our ideas and take care of our needs, values and relationships.

For this reason, I have sought to create a method to integrate these teachings into our daily lives.

In the Meditation of the Vortex of Energy I have joined the element of Ether in Qi, the vital energy that connects and binds the magnetic field, the earth beneath our feet, our heart center, expression and all our surroundings.

Some people feel a very strong connection with their families, while others feel a special attraction for humanitarian causes or spiritual matters. We find our harmony at the focal point, developing a balance between these two aspects. Some people have a directed destiny to one way or the other or both. The two forces, much like the yin and the yang, are different. Neither is better than the other. They complement each other. This duality can cause constant stress and internal conflict. We may feel caught between two paths. Our responsibility is to regularize our space and the relationship within this duality.

In Tantric Numerology, people who have numbers five and higher tend to be attracted by spiritual and community causes. People who mainly have numbers lower than number five can feel more attached to their family, emotional, material and traditional aspects.

Each person has their own way and their own life to manage. Ether connects all these aspects, without discrimination. The goal is to find happiness, well-being, purpose and to comfortably share space.The pursuit of happiness is a very noble path of acceptance, peace, compassion and inspiration. Yet what about choosing to be happy along the way, rather than setting happiness as an end goal? You can look for more enjoyable things to do and enjoy more greatly the things you do.

Ether supports the link between male and female energy, the yin and the yang. This energy travels freely and unconditionally. When we awaken our consciousness, we are moving with clarity, ease, and intention. We perceive this force without seeing it. It is invisible and yet very real.

When you rub your hands one against the other, and then you place the palm of your hands against each other, you feel a sensation of heat or tingling. If you perform this exercise regularly, the feeling will become increasingly strong. With regular practice, you can create forms that you can move and activate your vital energy.

Some people "see" this space. Some cameras have a level of extreme sensitivity that reveals this magnetic field, this energy on the screen and on photos. Dr. Korotkov has created GDV machine technology, which is very advanced. In upcoming illustrations, you will see the effect of the Meditation on the chakras and the energy field, illustrated by GDV photos.

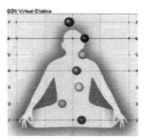 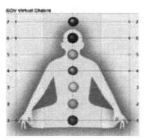

(pictures credit to Lydia Grosjean Switzerland)

This tool is very precise and sensitive to vibrations.

When people practice intensive sports or martial arts, they learn that when the physical body can no longer go on, the mind takes over. When the mind no longer follows, it is the spirit that takes over. The person is then in a trance, beyond the physical and directs their mind beyond their limits.

In 1992, Avi Grinberg, my professor of holistic reflexology and bodywork based on the Five Elements, initiated me to touch the Element of Ether. It was work at a distance from the body, specifically affecting the energy body, the magnetic field. These exercises are very intense and can awaken deep reactions in the person receiving them. It is an alignment that is very sensitive to the depths of the being, which affects the magnetic field subtly and all the other dimensions of the body.

Lifting the magnetism, the energy aspect in the Ether Element.

When this Element is strengthened, there is more electro-magnetism. We can also improve food quality by channeling this energy. Studying nutrition, I learned that smoothies should be consumed within 45 minutes after the fruits have been mixed. Beyond that time, there is much less electromagnetism and the properties of the fruits are already beginning to fade. The food no longer has the same nutritional quality. In practicing the Meditation, it enables this electromagnetism in the seven frequencies to reconnect and regenerate this fundamental energy present in every part of our body. Restoring and balancing the vital energy in our five bodies (physical, emotional, energy, psychological and spiritual) with consciousness and direction, brings a sensation of plenitude, alertness, and well-being.

One day, I showed the basic exercise mentioned above to an eight year old boy when he asked me about energy. To give him a better understanding of the concept of energy, I suggested he rub his two hands together, then stop and create a space between them. He said that he could feel heat and a tingling sensation, and he told me he could see slightly blurry colors, in waves, between his hands.

This observation showed that his third eye was open, that it had not yet been repressed with judgments and preconceptions. He was so impressed by this discovery that he wanted to share it with his father. When he approached him, his father was in conversation with friends. When his son arrived to share his discovery, he laughed and said that it was nothing; that it did not exist. The boy was disappointed, sad and confused. He came back to me to tell me that in fact, perhaps there was nothing, maybe it was just his imagination. I asked him, "What do you think really? In what do you want to believe?", He told me that he had felt something special between his hands and seen waves. It was beautiful and it had given him a feeling of well-being. I then suggested he believe in what he wanted and that we could keep it as a secret between us. Not everyone can see or perceive such things. If other people do not believe, it is ok, because everyone has their own perspective and chooses to think what they want. We therefore chose to keep this a secret between us until he meets other people who have similar levels of perception as him. We have the freedom to think what we like of what we see or sense.

Learning to trust what you feel reflects a healthy connection with the Element of Ether. When we make decisions based on faith, we open ourselves up to the path of the heart. These are moments of connection with our authentic nature, which reinforce this relationship. We can learn how to align our internal clock and venture carefully.

In seeking our star or our path, we are looking to access this energy and this guide within and around. The connection is sometimes stifled by fears, wounds and doubts. It can be difficult to access and you may feel some resistance. When we incorporate this voice, we can no longer go back. It is an awakening that affects us and gives us a sense of purpose, and responsibility which becomes difficult to deny after we awaken mindfulness.

People who regularly perform this Meditation choose a day and a precise and convenient schedule for them. This allows for a better integration and alignment of balance, and the activation of a certain frequency, intention and concentration. This energy binds us to the source of creation, to the light and brings us a sense of belonging and integration. It invites us to look at a goal beyond our ego or our conditioning. Ether has a particular importance in the Vortex of Energy Meditation. It is the Element that binds all the other Elements together. It is the source of the process and the golden, invisible string that connects us all.

Shamanic experience

One day, while I was in shamanic rituals, I was able to attend a very special event, when the shaman reconnected someone's life line. After a strong and intense Temazcal (sweat lodge), we all went to bathe in the river flowing down from the mountain. It was part of the ritual. We'd spent a few hours in the Inipi, an Indian tent where one sang, received lessons, broke free from toxins and trauma, and shared words of wisdom that had often come from our subconscious.

The Inipi ritual includes four passages, the four doors. At each crossing, the door is opened to receive some light and add a few more red volcanic stones in the center. At each opening of the door, the intensity, the heat, and the liberation become increasingly strong. It is a sacred process of purification and liberation. When we came out, we were all in a bit of a transcendental state. We walked down to the river to complete the process of purification in cold water.

At that time, a participant began to feel very weak. We helped him lie down on the edge of the river. His heart stopped for a few seconds. The shaman was just beside him. He approached the young man and reconnected the gold string through chanting and rituals. The young man then resumed consciousness. The shaman was very tired after this intervention. He said it was not something to do too often, because it meant intervening in another person's space. However, in this situation, it had been necessary. He reminded us that, thanks to fate, we had all been present at this time to support him energetically by sending out intention and prayers. There is always a certain mystery to consider as well as the intention and the energy of the group.

In the book written by Vladimir Megre, "Anastasia", the young woman shares her pure connection and authentic nature and its forces. It reminds us that every being has their own rhythm and destiny and that it is not good to abuse the powers of nature. It is best to respect nature's wisdom and destiny.

Combination of the mystery/spirituality and science

One day, I received a phone call from a person with whom I had worked and guided through consultations with the DHARMI Method (holistic healing and personal development). This woman had tried to become pregnant for years. As the natural method had not worked, she had tried different medical procedures. This was a very difficult time for her. However, during the process, she managed to become pregnant. She felt her body and her mind open during the last attempt at artificial fertilization. Following this meeting, I had no more news for a few months, until the day she called me from the hospital.

She informed me that her baby had been born prematurely, by caesarean section. She would have preferred to wait a little longer and allow a natural birth, but the doctors had told her it was important to do it more quickly for her safety and that of the child. The baby was therefore in intensive care for a few days, with machines that kept his lungs active so he could continue to breathe in order to survive. The child couldn't live without medical support and the doctors had seen no improvement so far. She had then thought of me. She wanted me to come and channel energy to help the process. I told her that I couldn't guarantee anything. If she wanted me to come to the hospital, she had to ask for the consent of her husband and the doctors. My role was to channel the vital energy to support the medical process and the family. I was very clear that this was not a therapy and this visit was additional to the other care that the newborn was receiving, as a prayer or meditation. They all gave their permission and approval.

The next morning, after preparation and a meditation, I went to find them at the hospital. I had to channel the energy through the parents. It was the only way. It was necessary to clarify an energy, the gap between the father and the mother to be able to allow the incarnation of the soul of the child in its physical body. In fact, we needed to unite our prayers, our thoughts and our best wishes. I then asked the parents to participate. I focused my attention, intention and visualization. Prayer actually means opening your heart and your mind with a positive intention and unconditional love (agape). They were very receptive, even the father who was very puzzled because he did not believe at all in these things.

With lots of attention and concentration, I managed to visualize the passage of energy. It was a specific moment when the parents and the child found the click of connection, love and union. At the time where the symbol of light appeared, I felt that the child would live. I told them that all was well. They felt a space of openness and confidence in life within themselves.

The next day, I received news that the child was better. A few days later, he could breathe without the support of the medical equipment. The situation evolved well. He was being followed by doctors, and his body was receptive to the treatments. His condition quickly improved and in a matter of days his family could take him home.

This experience was a revelation on the complementarity between technology, love, union and prayer in a Western and Eastern medicine/approach. Sometimes our prayers need technology and eastern medicine to support an event. Sometimes, technology and eastern medicine needs prayers to support independence and detachment of certain machinery and certain medications.

Experience of Letting Go

I once supported the personal development process of a woman in her forties who had been trying to have a child for many years. She had tried all sorts of invasive medical treatments to give herself every chance possible, but it still hadn't worked, and she had become increasingly frustrated.

She contacted me to help her find the strength to redirect her attention and energy. She had gone through many episodes of mourning over the previous few years, and with each disappointment, she had increasingly lost confidence and become ever more focused on her goal. Gradually, she learnt to find peace and regain inner strength. She followed a path that guided her in a new direction, while honoring her intent and her inner voice. She began to let go, thanks to new enlightenments and perspectives that she humbly opened herself up to. As she accepted and explored new possibilities, she began to regain confidence, and has found greater serenity and self-esteem.

Once she had finally let go, and began on a new path, regaining confidence in herself, this woman was given a new opportunity to try to have a child. After thinking about it carefully, she decided to accept this last chance.

A few weeks later, I felt the urge to phone her to ask for news. She told me that she had just come out of a doctor's appointment and she had just seen and heard the first heartbeat in her womb. That day was close to her 49th day of pregnancy, the time when «life» takes form in the fetus according to Buddhist philosophy.

We continued the process, and I accompanied her on her journey in life, which continues to amaze us, step after step, day after day. There is a certain destiny beyond our control, and this destiny is bound by a fine line to our intent, our mission, and our aspirations.

The mystery of the universal consciousness gives us a sense of belonging beyond judgment, attachment, or fear. It is a space of liberation that is pure and true in its form, color, and vibration. It reminds us that we are all one, but that we are also each unique. I have always been struck by certain discoveries and encounters I have had with ancestral traditions and cultures. These dances, rituals, and healing bear great wisdom, and I have a lot of respect for these different philosophies.

Over the course of my experience, I became aware of a real gap between today's society and the wisdom of our ancestors. But despite this gap, I felt that everything was connected.

During some of my travels, I had visions of ancient civilizations. It was as though I had already experienced or studied them. Perhaps I was listening to the memory still present in the air we breathe. A wisdom that we have access to when we open ourselves up to receive information beyond words. The more I discovered different cultures, traditions, and perspectives, the more I realized that they were all related. Gradually I brought all this knowledge together to create the DHARMI Method, (a clear Map to guide you on your life's journey). It was a natural step on my journey.

All these paths are authentic, profound, filled with wisdom, and based on some kind of science. They can provide a sensation of indescribable plenitude. Each path uniquely enriches those who follow it.

~ Chapter 5 ~

OVERVIEW OF THE DIFFERENT PATHS

The Bandhas in the Vortex of Energy meditation

The Sanskrit word bandha is derived from Indian philosophy and yoga, meaning bond, lock, muscle control, or union.

I have explored many paths and methods in search of balance, well-being, and consciousness. I have sometimes even experienced sensations as powerful out of body experiences and trances. But the return to «reality» was not always harmonious. The return to society and daily life was difficult. A growing gap began to develop between the spiritual world and my daily life, and this gap became hard to live with. I felt a real duality between freedom from all material constraint and the necessities of human life in today's society.

I have met several people who have had very powerful experiences, or out of body sensations, and who have found it hard to come back again. Some people chose to stop meditating after such events, while others felt an increasing need for spiritual retreats. In some cases, they detached themselves from their families, their fundamental values, and their bases. Both worlds are important for our balance and evolution. They complement each other perfectly. But we need to find their point of union and balance.

Incorporating the bandhas into DHARMI meditations reinforces the connection with several points of attachment to the physical body.

Losing yourself in meditation, without any direction or point of reference is like launching yourself into space without a parachute. Our mind works like a parachute, it fulfills its role best when it is open. But it is important to stay attached to it so you can direct it and maintain a healthy connection.

Using the bandhas allows you to anchor yourself more clearly and to maintain control while allowing yourself to let go. Being well anchored improves the flow of energy in our daily lives. The bandhas are internal locks that keep the energy contained. They are anchor points. Understanding the bandhas is key to receiving the full benefits of meditation.

Energetically, the bandhas create opposing forces like the polarities of a battery with energy flowing between them. They provide stability and a sense of security beyond external attachments.

Each bandha has well defined properties and can help you regulate your internal, hormonal, sexual, and digestive systems, and so forth. They are the keys to light, fluid, and harmonious expression.

The Four Bandhas:

Mula Bandha

Is the root or the foundation lock. It provides an anchor and a strong and healthy connection to our roots by closing the base of the trunk. It is directly linked to the Earth element and helps to contain it, to support the physical body, and to bind us to our sexual energy. When we clarify our relationship with this space, we learn to direct and contain our sexuality for improved creativity and well-being.

I consider that sexual energy is not simply limited to sex or physical love, it is also the fundamental, tantric energy of creation, creativity, and enlightenment. It is the basic force at the source of being, which opens us up to prosperity.

This bandha also reminds us of discipline and our basic needs, to respect our space and that of those around us. When we are well anchored, it also brings us a sense of respect for fundamental commitments.

The Mula Bandha can open us up to the true source of creation and being.

Uddiyana Bandha

Is the lock located in the area of the solar plexus and the diaphragm.

This bandha is the fire of the digestive system and its related functions. It tones the organs and helps them to function better. It also helps to dispel anxiety and stress.

In the DHARMI Method, this bandha is considered the link between the elements of water and fire, and it helps to balance emotions, feelings and actions. It supports decision making, will power, selectivity, and stress relief.

It also helps strengthen the deep muscles of the lower back.

Jalandhara Bandha

Is the lock located in the area of the throat and neck. It has an important influence on the **nadis**, and it balances the thyroid.

It is located between fire and air, and it allows us to measure and channel our communication, feelings, voice, and strength of expression.

Its purpose is to redirect the ascending energy towards the spine. It connects you with the energy of air and ether, and allows you to contain your energy while opening up a space of consciousness and clarity.

In Sanskrit, Jalandhara jal means throat, jalan is a net, and dharan a stream or flow. This bandha controls the circulation of energy in the nerves and blood vessels of the neck, and regulates the endocrine system.

Maha Bandha

Is the lock that creates the connection between the first three bandhas. It is the master lock.

The exercises with the different bandhas can help to make you a better runner, swimmer, or athlete, and help to balance your health.

The Three Gunas in the Vortex of Energy Meditation

The word *Guna* comes from Sanskrit. It represents qualities, states of being, and properties.

When we speak of being *«tamasic»*, we are referring to a space of laziness and slowness. It can be seen when people choose to stay in their comfort zone and continue with what is familiar without making any effort to try and move beyond it, even when it isn't healthy for them. The word tamas means inertia, obscurity, or heaviness.

Resisting or forcing things is termed *«rajastic»*. It can be seen in controlling behavior and a search for challenges, or when someone tries to push or force changes under stress and pressure. Rajas means passion, desire, and strength.

When we are in a *«sattvic»* space, we achieve a state of ease and enlightenment. This makes us feel confident while remaining very alert. It can be seen in the attention and clarity we show in our actions. There is no resistance or pressure. We can then advance in respect of the natural cycles of evolution on our journey. Sattva represents purity and truth.

The three gunas are all a part of our lives at different times. Being aware of and recognizing these different states helps to brings us back to our central point.

During the Vortex of Energy Meditation, the participants identify the rajastic, tamasic, and sattvic elements within themselves. They can then incorporate them into their personal development process so that they have more tools which to balance themselves and follow a path of evolution.

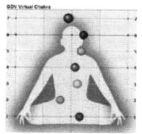

The chakras in the Vortex of Energy

The chakras are energy vortexes that are in alignment with the central channel, known as the *sushumna* in yoga philosophy. Clarifying and activating the central channel with vital energy, visualization, and the palms of the hands helps to directly align the chakras. It is like a magnetic effect that brings them naturally back to their central point and alignment.

Alignment of the chakras before and after the Vortex of Energy Meditation:

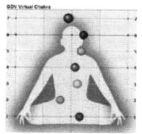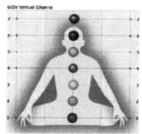

(pictures credit to Lydia Grosjean Switzerland)

Activating Vital Energy in Meditation

Qigong is a traditional Chinese practice based on understanding and directing our vital energy. The word Qi means vital energy, and the word Gong means activation or mastery. The discipline is based on slow movements and breaths that support good health and a balanced life.

My experience in Qigong has been beneficial both as a discipline and as a healing process.

I first discovered Qigong in the late 80s, in Biel, a small town in Switzerland near my childhood village. With each class, I learned how to access a powerful, subtle, and very deep force within me. It was strange to discover that such serene and delicate movements could bring such inner strength and general well-being.

I later had the opportunity to resume my Qigong practice during my time in China and then in the United States.

When I visited the south of China without a map or a tourist guide, there was no internet at the time. So, I guided myself through the encounters I had each day. I was planning on discovering Chinese traditions on my way to Vietnam.

I experienced travelling in Chinese trains and buses. Early in the morning, the city parks were full of people performing martial arts exercises: Tai chi, Qigong, and other practices. Their discipline in life was very strong and motivating.

While I was staying in a small village, one family was particularly kind to me and prepared a traditional meal in my honor. It was very disturbing, as I had to swallow pieces of snake out of respect for their tradition.

Some of the experiences I had were very intense and awakened fears that I had to quickly channel in order to remain attentive to my surroundings. I realized that the fears and emotions that awakened adrenaline allowed me to stay very alert. This is important when traveling alone in remote and sometimes dangerous places.

One day, in a village near Nannin, I met some twins and their father. They were masters of Qigong and perhaps the only family in the area who spoke English. I was fortunate to be able to share some enriching experiences with them.

They explained some aspects of their practice to me and the therapeutic process based on Qigong. They were also very curious to find out more about the other therapeutic approaches that I had studied in the West. Their father introduced me to aspects of Qigong in its martial art form. Watching him, I could perceive the very special and beneficial power it had.

We spent a few days together, and they recommended I go to another village to continue my experience and get closer to my next destination, Vietnam. In the next village, I discovered a Buddhist temple located within a mountain. It was an unforgettable and almost unreal experience.

Eight years later, after practicing meditation, coaching, and shamanism, I resumed contact with Tai Chi and Qigong masters. I devoted several years of learning and experience to incorporating the basics of this practice and did training as a Qigong instructor.

The movements are very pure, centered, and focused, and I have incorporated some key aspects of this discipline into the Vortex of Energy Meditation to strengthen the power of intention. Directing our Qi during meditation facilitates cleansing and the release of physical, emotional, and mental toxins.

For me, mental toxins are preconceived judgments and beliefs that are harmful to our well-being and the well-being of others. Physical toxins or stresses can take the form of viruses, fat gain, tension, or other symptoms where energy no longer flows in a healthy way. Activating our vital energy opens our circulation and balances our emotional, psychological, and physical body. The method requires a lot of concentration and releases the stress accumulated over different frequencies and dimensions. I consider it an active meditation.

We learn to feel the movements and their effects on our body and mind. Through channeled breathing and serene movements, we open space for a feeling of warmth. Our thoughts become clearer and we become more attentive. With regular discipline, we become more spontaneous in our actions and decisions. This force needs to be well channeled so we can use it for positive intentions based on compassion, love, and light, for our own well-being and that of those around us.

In Qigong, each dantian is a vital energy center and a place of alchemy. These energy centers are like the chakras. Qigong focuses on three dantian centers: one in the belly, one in the heart space and rib cage, and one in the head located near the third eye. The movements create connections and circulation between each energy center.

Over the course of my experience, I began to feel that the bandhas were bonds that connect these centers together and help the energy circulate. When the bandhas are well activated, they become the containers for these circulating energies.

People who do the Vortex of Energy Meditation regularly learn to incorporate these aspects to better channel their energy and intent. This requires a lot of concentration and an ability to let go in order to awaken particularly subtle potential and levels of consciousness.

Incorporating Sacred Geometry into the Vortex of Energy Meditation

Everything that honors nature's wisdom and the law of the universe can be considered sacred. Humankind, nature, animals, minerals, all living beings and forms are sacred. When I speak about sacred geometry, I include geometry, symbols, forms, and shapes that are aligned with natural laws. When I speak about sacredness, this means that all creation deserves respect, compassion, and its space to be.

You can incorporate certain aspects of sacred geometry into the DHARMI Method. The wisdom of nature and the laws of the universe are our main guides, examples to inspire creativity and help us evolve on our path. They are one of the ingredients in the recipe of meditation that help ensure we have a delicious, beneficial, and enjoyable experience!

Why «sacred» geometry? Because the laws of the universe and the wisdom of nature are considered sacred. Human beings, nature, animals, minerals, and all beings and living forms are sacred. When I refer to sacred geometry, this includes all symbols, forms, and natural states that are in alignment with the laws of the universe, evolution, and nature. We can see it in the arrangement and layout of all sorts of spaces, in architecture, and in many other aspects of our daily lives.

Every step, every experience, and every thought opens up new paths in our labyrinth, our journey in life. A thought can lead us in a totally new direction. A look or a smile can change our lives. A movement can completely redirect our future. But we are often too focused on our expectations, projections, and conditioning. We let ourselves be overwhelmed by stress, the trend for consumerism, and habits and influences that lead us away from our center and our intention. Meditation creates a little space within us in which we can breathe and recenter. When we focus on our feelings and our ways of functioning, we discover spaces and realities that open up new doors for us. This requires a different perspective; we must be calm and attentive to the constant movements and lessons on our path in life.

Meditation helps us absorb the information and lessons that we can learn from our experiences. It is always good to take some time to reconnect with ourselves and appreciate what we have learned over the course of the day.

I think that all forms of creation deserve a certain respect. Philosophers, researchers, scientists, and physicists all have different notions of creation, and each perspective contains its own truth. I believe a certain mystery exists behind every form of creation. Depending on your own tradition, beliefs, scientific research, and view point, you can call it what you like; the source of divine life, the sacred spring, God, Buddha....

The combination of the two forces and energies allows for creation and manifestation, the passage from space into matter. The very perspective of feminine and masculine energy is relative, as is that of yin and yang. It all depends on the view point from which you consider them.

It is the point of union that creates energy and manifestation. Life is born from the union and complementarity between two forces. The one cannot exist without the other, it is like the story of the chicken and the egg.

At the moment of conception, the masculine energy of the father unites with the feminine energy of the mother to bring about fertilization - conception. There is no life without the union of polarities.

Energetically, the union of these two forces forms two circles which unite to produce the eye, the central point of creation and materialization, in its center. It resembles the fish symbol that the Christians drew on the ground to recognize each other.

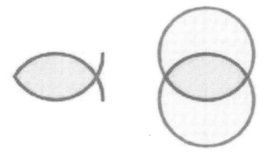

We have both these forces within us. The key is to find a balance that allows for harmony and a healthy relationship between the two forces. The connection between these two energies opens us up to creativity and creates the spark and source of inspiration.

We are born in this space of union and love that forms our cocoon for the entire course of our lives. Permanent expansion takes its source from its central point of creation, like the flower of life. [symbolo Flor de la Vida]

These two great circles are in continuous circulation, connecting us with our surroundings. The cycles of exchange of giving and receiving are in a continuous, harmonious, and complete state of connection. Our Energy Vortex is at the center and opens the path to abundance in *quantum* energy. If we try to separate ourselves from this point of union, we lose our connection with the natural cycles and hence with our surroundings and environment, which can lead to a sense of isolation. On the other hand, if we are too attached to these external points of union and if we do not focus our energy on our center, it can lead to co-dependencies that create imbalances.

Enlightenment and each new cycle originates from the center, opening us up to a sense of harmony and fulfillment, while balancing the different frequencies. It is the source of inspiration and creation.

I believe we are all spiritual beings. We are given our physical body to allow us to manifest and reflect an intention, a form of expression and creation. We all have different needs and motivations.

We live in a continuous state of exchange between our inner universe and our outer universe.

But how can we find a balance between these two universes?

And where is the point of union between illusion and reality?

Clarity comes along the way. We cannot discover anything without advancing. We cannot learn without exploring and seeking. The fear of making mistakes limits our ability to evolve and succeed. We cannot know where the path will lead until we visualize it and take it.

The triangle and the hexagram

The triangle illustrates the trinity. I have incorporated the notion of the trinity into the DHARMI Map in the form of the three paths: The Cycle of Evolution, the Vortex of Energy Meditation, and the Cycle of Energy through the Elements.

In the Vortex of Energy Meditation, the two triangles correspond to specific elements; pyramid symbols that facilitate the expression of resonance. The heart is at the center, symbolizing connection with the source and the reflection of the Divine in our physical, corporal, and temporal forms.

The symbol of two unified triangles forms the *hexagram* found in the Jewish *Merkabah*, the Star of David, and many other symbols such as the Hindu *Yantra* and Buddhist philosophies.

DHARMI® Meditation helps us incorporate an intention at its source, in the heart. The first vibration of the sound «AUM» is that of materialization. These two triangles are represented in the symbol of the Vortex of Energy Meditation.

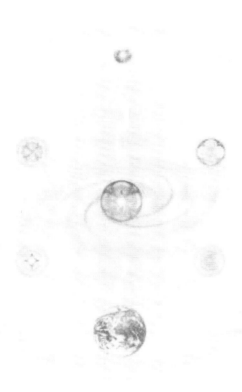

The central channel and the union at the origin of creation

Starting from the principle of the two forces (the two polarities, the yin and the yang, the feminine and the masculine) that unite to create life, Vesica piscis is the union that allows for creation. It is from this central point that we can channel our intention and direct our lives.

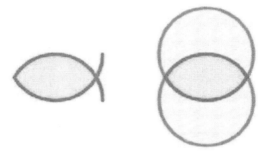

We create our reality from the central channel that unites these two points of union. (symbol) This line forms the central axis of meditation.

In the tradition of Yoga, three *nadis* are the reference points. The first, *sushumna* (Sanskrit), is a central channel. It is the link between the chakras, which are a series of seven energy centers. The sushumna distributes the vital energy (prana) through our organs and our being. This channel allows the connection with the other two *nadis*: the feminine force *(Ida)* and the masculine force *(Pingala)*.

To achieve a general balance, I have considered the relationship between our two nervous systems, the central nervous system is particularly logical, while the enteric nervous system is intuitive and is based on emotional intelligence.

The center, which represents the union between the two forces, channels creative energy. In Tantric philosophy, sexual energy does not exist purely for sex as such, but for communication with the universe and the source of creation. The balance of the chakras and the five bodies, channels sexual energy toward creation in its purest and most essential form. Our visions and aspirations are manifested through this energy and creative force.

We are spiritual beings having a human experience; it is a constant learning process throughout our lives. We sometimes feel a rift between our human reality and our deepest essence. Over our few years of incarnation, we are given the opportunity to experience (karma) and integrate (dharma). We can choose to move forward on a path that reflects our intentions and values in our expression and relationships.

What is our truth? What is our reason for living?

When we open the third eye and purify our being of trauma and resistance, we can find the path of the heart. We are all unique and we all react differently to our life experiences. We are all influenced from conception by a range of factors, our surroundings, our metabolism, and our culture. But we have infinite possibilities for our emotional expression, perspectives, and approach.

If we follow our heart, our intention, and our vision, it will naturally lead us to the right place. They know better than our ego. Our reason for living is not an ultimate goal, but a path, a way of life, a way of moving forward!

The voice of the ego screams while the voice of wisdom whispers.

Some of us have been programmed since childhood with a linear way of thinking that creates a sense of security. Linear thoughts make it possible for us to have reference points that are very rational, tangible, and clear. But opening our minds in a broader sense allows us to better absorb experiences at a holistic level. This openness also gives us a clearer overall perception of life.

The DHARMI Cycles of Evolution

When we follow the course of our lives with intention in the right direction, we feel in alignment with our surroundings. We need to learn to let go so we may navigate our way through life with harmony and confidence.

One of our main sources of stress comes from attachment to our fears, which causes personal blockages in ourselves and towards those around us. Another source of stress comes from our expectations or projections. Our surroundings also sometimes awaken stress at a physical, emotional, or psychological level.

To allow the energy to flow and to find a space of integrity, we must balance the Five Elements within us. This process creates alignment on a new frequency in the constant evolution of life.

Our interpretations of many of our experiences are deeply rooted in our emotional, mental, and physical memory. This memory can be revived at any time in the present. Our beliefs attached to the memory then generate a direct reaction that reproduces similar circumstances. Our resonance and expression arise from this reference point, which is linked to our past history.

Our negative ego is so powerful that it influences our subconscious and seeks to be right. That is why we attract and are attracted by similar situations. These reactions to fear and attachment create vicious circles, whereas when we open ourselves up to new perspectives and the voice of wisdom, we open to the natural flow and harmonious continuation of life cycles.

Our muscular memory, emotional memory, and way of seeing things is forged by our deep beliefs and experiences. If we attach ourselves to our pain and fear, we build a bulwark around our heart and the source of creation within us.

Our thoughts and viewpoints are reflected in the Air element. Our actions, motivations, and feelings are present in the Fire element. Our emotions and relationships are found in the Water element. Our physical health and discipline are manifested in the Earth element. And our inspirations, faith, and intention are present in the Ether element.

We can open our path to a different frequency by aligning with a positive intention. When our shell or our mask begins to slow down our movement and our expression, it creates a lag that manifests itself in stress. By following the Map, we can become aware of these blockages and clarify our reference points to open new doors on our journey.

Is it we who find the solution or the solution that finds us?

A friend once told me that it was always possible to find a solution, but our impatience to find it causes a lot of stress and frustration. *Is it really we who find the solution, or the solution that finds us?*

The Map opens us to new perspectives that allow us to experience new horizons. It awakens perceptions beyond the linear mode of thought. The process of creating this methodology has been a gradual one. I followed my intention and my quest for clarity along my journey, and they have led me to decipher and now to pass on these key elements in our personal development.

It was not a goal I had set for myself, but a mystery that was revealed to me during the experiences I had on my journey. It is the accumulation of my life experiences. I have humbly explored, while remaining true to myself and following my intention. And the doors of my labyrinth continue to open and reveal many surprises. My journey continues. It is with great pleasure that I share my personal experience to contribute to other people's development and well-being.

Jennifer* had tried several coaching methods oriented toward her professional goals. When she followed a series of five DHARMI sessions, she clarified her intention, and this clarity allowed her to align her seven frequencies with confidence and determination. This inner harmony was reflected in her actions, and she was able to achieve professional and personal goals beyond her expectations.

Focusing on an objective based on ego, fear, or attachment can take us away from our values. We then lose the substance of pure and positive intention. This amounts to reinforcing unfulfilled expectations and conditioning. Our reason for living is revealed and becomes clearer day by day when we focus on our intention and honor our path and the laws of the universe. It is not really us (ego) who finds our destiny. It is our destiny that is revealed to us along our path when we learn to let go and move forward with confidence.

The transition from experience *(karma)* to integration *(dharma)* opened me up to the possibility of guiding people with the DHARMI Map and helping them clarify their own paths.

Life is a constant evolution. It is the reflection of love, the inner flame that shines and illuminates our steps. As soon as we stop movement, we prevent the flow of vital energy from being recycled and renewed. Sometimes, when we experience a failure or the loss of a loved one we feel something die within ourselves. The most difficult part to handle is when the pain stifles our inner flame. We lose our connection with our inspiration, our dreams, and our vital energy.

This meditation sharpens your consciousness step after step, breath after breath, dream after dream. You will explore and discover. And you will encounter surprises at every stage. When you stop, and allow space for stillness, you can find serenity and absorb your experiences. Then you can move on with greater integrity in your achievements by seeking the projection of pure love.

I wish you a journey full of inspiration, enlightenment, and discoveries!

~ Chapter 6 ~

EXAMPLE THEMES
AND INTENTIONS FOR THE PRACTICE OF THE
VORTEX OF ENERGY MEDITATION

In this section, you will find examples with specific the-mes on which you can focus on in alignment with the moon cycles or other occasions that you choose from to practice, or to facilitate people through the Meditation. Before beginning the Meditation, you will clarify your map and focus on those specific aspects during the practice. During the practice you will receive insights that you can write down and include in your notes after completing the meditation. You will continue to focus on that intention and alignment for seven days.

The North Hemisphere Spring Equinox is a symbolic time of transition in which we move in the direction of the Elements for a harmonious and aligned meditation practice.

East: Water Element

South: Earth Element

West: Air Element

North: Fire Element

At that same time, people in the Southern hemisphere are experiencing the shift for the Autumn, Fall Equinox, with the element of Air in the East. This is a reminder of the imper-manence and constant evolution on our journey. If it is waxing moon, I recommend you focus on the expansion form turning clockwise using the theme over the next few days of Blooming.

What quality and intention do you wish to see blooming this Spring?

Clearing space - Waning moon and every four years during a leap day.

The waning moon reminds us to release attachments and to clear space and time. A leap day is a good opportunity to take a leap of faith. The Vortex of Energy Meditation done counter-clockwise will support your journey.

Ether: Personal intention (compassion, detachment, clarity, space and harmony)

Air: Is there a certain thought that takes you away from your priorities, that distracts your mind and clouds your mental sky?

Fire: Do you notice any feelings or desires that are repressed? What holds you back?

Water: Are there any bursts of emotions that are difficult for you to channel or master?

Earth: Are you too busy? Do you have too much on your plate at this time? Can you let go of something to make more space and time to create?

Let your intention be in peace and alignment with all seven frequencies, making use of the «clearing form», which encourages acceptance, compassion, gratitude and letting go of what holds you back, or is not supporting your positive intention at this time of your life. Be in tune, supporting each other, united in our uniqueness.

Full Moon Oneness

The moon is shining brighter and brighter every night, soon to reach its fullness. May it be a time to shine to your full potential, honoring your intention with clarity and integrity in all Seven Frequencies.

I personally have practiced the Vortex of Energy clockwise centering form of the Meditation. It felt like I was the strongest, purest, and lightest I have ever been. I felt fully embraced in the vibration of my intention, at one within and all around. By practicing this way too, you may feel connected to the life source, the moon, people, community and environment.

Moving through the cycles *(Refer to the book Elements on the Journey)*:

I learned from my study of holistic foot reflexology, that all humans experience several main stages of evolution, based on the Elements:

Earth – Learning survival skills with first steps, first words, basic hygiene, from birth to 3-4 years.

Water – Gaining further emotional development, beginning to use more developed words and form of expression, relating with others from ages 10-12 years.

Fire - Developing self-esteem, individuality, personality and ego during the teenage years, up to 18-20 years.

Air – Becoming an independent thinker, exploring options and different interests, engaging in studies to clarify your direction and vision from 26 years onward.

Many people repeat cycles after that. Yet, we have the opportunity to continue to grow as we mature. This is a time where we evolve through different cycles rather than turning in vicious circles. It requires dedication to pass from one cycle to another and to take a leap of faith towards your true calling.

Ether: What is an intention or purpose that you would like to empower and nurture at this time?

Air: Clarify a thought or vision that encourages you to move forward and to open your mind to new opportunities.

Fire: How can you build up your confidence? Which of your gifts is calling for your attention at this time?

Water: How can you channel your emotions in a way that supports your intention?

Earth: How much time, dedication and space can you invest in your development and the intention you aspire to experience?

Moving clockwise will help you honor your personal and universal cycle.

Focus on these themes while completing the moon cycle:

Opening up – Waxing moon

As we enter the waxing moon cycle, a time of harmony and inspiration, it is a time to practice the Vortex of Energy Meditation clockwise. It is a time to open up and to unveil new possibilities. The intention is one of openness. I suggest you clarify the intention you'd like to open up and empower at this time.

Earth: How can you organize your space and time for the manifestation and embodiment of your intention?

Air: Which perspective and affirmation reflects openness?

Fire: What is the intensity and rhythm that will support this intention?

Water: How can you share with openness honoring healthy values and relationships?

Clarity and Surrender - Waning Moon

There is a Japanese tradition that suggests clearing and cleaning your space at the end of each year. The more we clear space, the more space we have for new things. It takes faith and courage to surrender, which is a beautiful intention during this time of the waning moon.

A reminder that the setup for the 4 Elements during Winter is:

East – Earth: Are there any material aspects to let go of? Are there any responsibilities or weights on your spirit that you can lighten by allowing them to be lifted?

North – Water: Are there any emotions that you have repressed that you can now clear? Are you feeling overwhelmed?

West – Fire: Did you put off expressing any of your feelings? Are you overactive and need some time and space to balance the intensity of your fire and your expression of it?

South - Air: Is your mind distracted or overloaded with thoughts that preoccupy you? Can you clarify your mind?

Ether connects them all and helps you to honor a space of clarity, surrender to who you are, in your truth, in your heart, in the here and now.

Full Moon Oneness

With the enlightening energy of the Full Moon and the Winter Solstice, we focus on Oneness.

The shift of the seasons invites you to experience a shift in the position of the Elements. Winter is mainly reflected by the element of Earth, so the East rising direction will be reflected with the Earth Element through this season of hibernation, resting and nurturing our foundations.

East – Earth (during Winter time)

North – Water

West – Fire

South – Air

In this time of Oneness, I suggest using the intention of Abundance (Ether)

East/Earth – This is supportive of growth, community, time and space for abundance to grow and manifest,

South/Air – We expand, we blossom, we allow thoughts and perspective that flows from the Me to the We during this time of oneness.

West/Fire – Giving space for warmth, leadership and motivation to uplift the energy with leadership and clear actions for all.

North/Water – Sharing the greatness of abundance, being one with all within and around, feeling the water flowing, connecting the drops, from the rivers into the big ocean.

The Full Moon Centering Expanding form of the Vortex of Meditation will support your journey to Oneness.

Full Moon –Priorities & Manifestation

Ether – Personal intention related to manifestation and priorities.

Air - What are your main priorities when it comes to your ideas and dreams? What would you like to make come into being?

Fire - Which actions can support you in maintaining that direction and focus? What is your main trait of character, gift or talent you would like to empower and develop?

Water - Which relationships would you like to prioritize and make stronger? What level of relationships do you seek?

Earth - How can you create the space, time and resources to nurture the vision and idea that you'd like to manifest?

The New Moon – Planting New Seeds

Here we practice the Vortex of Energy Meditation in the centering form, counterclockwise, to plant a new seed with intention, giving space for a clear positive intention to flourish.

In each direction, you will nurture this intention with the respective Element, and align all the frequencies with the intention of your choice. Tune into the resonance and vibration of your instrument, allowing the quantum flow with grace and bliss.

Mercury Retrograde with a waning moon - Selection

It is time to practice selection. Mercury Retrograde periods remind us to select what we wish to keep and of what we wish to let go. This process is not only about external things, people or conditions. It is also about our own habits and thought processes.

I suggest that you clarify your intention and the aspects in which you can benefit from some selectivity.

Air (East): Can you be more selective with some thoughts or where you focus your attention and from where you get your intellectual stimulation (news, reading, movies, studies, etc.)?

Fire (North): Are there any actions that you can focus on with more selectivity and clarity? Are you doing things just to keep being busy? It can be better to actually do nothing, rather than trying to appear busy by doing something that wastes your precious, and finite time.

Water (West): Are there any emotions you have repressed? Relationships that you feed into that are not aligned with your intention or truth?

Earth (South): It can be a good time to clear a closet in your home and to let go material things you do not need anymore. It is also the perfect time to do a cleanse of your body.

New Moon –Alignment and Renewal

Your intention should be to consider where you are, renew that which serves you and align yourself with positive thoughts and actions.

Ether: It is now time to create space for expansion and the empowerment of your positive intention.

Air: Breathe your intention in and out, like the wind clearing and directing your mind. What is an affirmation or mantra that can support the expansion and integration of your intention?

Fire: Feel the warmth in your heart honoring your purpose. Can you take the role with integrity and express yourself from that intention with confidence?

Water: Flow with the water, become that flow and grace. How can you channel your emotions creatively to reflect that intention with harmony in your relationships?

Earth: Manifest and embody your intention. Respect your space, time and the temple in which you live. Create a strong foundation and base for your intention to manifest and grow harmoniously.

Ending of the Year: Clarification and Clearing

At the end of the year, it is a good time for clearing and completing cycles.

I suggest you focus on an intention you would like to clarify.

Air: Observe what your thoughts and expectations are concerning your intention and clarify your mind.

Fire: Reminds you to be clear in your expression and the role you take to reflect your intention.

Water: comes into consideration to honor your emotions and channel them clearly. It is a good time to clarify your emotions and relationships.

Earth: asks you to apply clarity to your space, time and body. Organize yourself to support a healthy body and lifestyle that is in tune with your intention.

Ether is the integration and clear intention of your choice.

Direction and Intention -The Vortex of Energy Meditation

When contemplating the theme of "Shining with Contentment" consider:

Air: What vision, idea or project could support you to shine?

Fire: What action could you take to make it happen?

Water: Which relationships could support the manifestation of this vision?

Earth: What time could you dedicate to this vision?

Here are some of the benefits you can receive through this active Meditation with their respective Element:

Earth Element – Physical

- Releases toxins and stress
- Supports the healing process after an injury, swelling, pinched nerve or ailment

- Releases chronic symptoms such as headaches, urinary tract infections, and back pain

- Improves body posture and the quality of sleep

- Strengthens the immune system and vital energy

Water Element – Emotional

- Balances emotions and supports channeling emotions with intention

- Releases emotional attachments

- Develops intuition and emotional intelligence

- Clarifies emotional response and response mechanisms in relationships

- Clears fear and heals emotional traumas

Fire Element – Feelings of self-esteem

- Strengthens self-confidence and self-esteem

- Acknowledges your feelings, desires and gifts

- Uplifts energy and motivation

- Clarifies the direction and intensity of your actions, behavior and personality roles with clarity and intention

- Develops leadership

Air Element – Mind

- Clarifies the mind

- Develops the potential for concentration, visualization and focus

- Clears reflection

- Awakens mindfulness, clarity of core beliefs, perspectives and affirmations

- Clarifies and strengthens the magnetic field

- Aligns the chakras

- Releases stress through acceptance, forgiveness, compassion and gratitude

- Integrates your intention and values

- Well-being and liberation of blockages or resistances

- Receptivity to synchronicities and spontaneity in daily life aligned with intention and frequency - An expanded capacity for alertness, compassion and conscious alignments in your life

- Activates vital energy and connection to the Divine source

- A clear, nurtured and expanded energy and magnetic field

- Aligns your personal dharma with the universal dharma

- Confidence to follow your life purpose

Below are pictures taken with a Gas Discharge Visualization Technology, GDV Machine, created by Dr. Constantine Korotkov. These pictures have been taken of a woman who had a bad fall on the stairs at her home and who noticed a strong imbalance in her energy after that experience. She chose to do the Vortex of Energy Meditation to heal her trauma and body pain and balance her energy.

Picture of the magnetic field before and after the Vortex of Energy Meditation:

 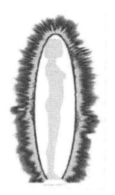

~ Chapter 7 ~

EXPERIENCE AND TESTIMONIES

This chapter shares the experience of people who have practiced the Vortex of Energy Meditation. Their names have been changed for privacy purposes.

After doing some personal development sessions, Jose* took part in a group meditation session. He had undergone some symbolic changes in his family life. His children had grown up and left home, and he had been through a difficult separation. He needed to affirm his values and responsibilities to be able to move forward on his path.

«During the meditation, I felt a very strong energy, and I noticed that my masculine and feminine energies were out of balance. I also noticed that the right and left sides of my brain began to balance during the practice. Since that seminar, I've carried on doing the Vortex of Energy Meditation on a daily basis. And I've noticed that I've become aligned with my intention. I'm more in harmony with those around me, I'm alert, and I can feel a more balanced flow in my life.»

While he was going through a career change, Danny* took part in regular meditation sessions. He wanted to share what he observed:

«I began doing the Vortex of Energy Meditation to resolve my self-doubt, to clarify my negative thoughts, and to align myself with an intention focused on well-being and balance. The meditation practice has made me more self-confident. I've become aware of the interaction between the different elements and of an internal language that I was not familiar with. It has made me more alert and helped me to develop more positive relationships with those around me. I have also learned to open up to opportunities that come my way with confidence and clarity.

By practicing the Vortex of Energy Meditation on a daily basis, I've been able to align more each day with the tone of my perception and learn how to handle situations better. To do this, I began focusing on clear and positive intentions towards myself and those around me. By regularly centering myself, I've been able to keep my energy focused, and it has opened up new possibilities for me. I can now recognize my old patterns from a new reference point, and I can acknowledge their presence and influence without giving them the energy and attention that would increase their power while weakening mine. Instead, I focus on my intention and my new perspective, and my magnetic field purifies my toxic thoughts and energies.

A new space has opened up in my personal development, and the opportunities that present themselves are in alignment with my new vibration and intention.»

Danny* continues to practice meditation on his own now and does regular DHARMI sessions online to help him follow his path with clarity and direction. This allows him to re-center.

During a trip to Miami, a Brazilian woman, Maryann*, attended a seminar and did some meditation. One of her friends, who knew that Maryann was experiencing a lot of stress and that she needed to gain perspective on an important decision in her life, recommended the approach to her.

«I decided to do the Vortex of Energy Meditation, because I was going through a time of great stress and doubt that was reflected in my relationships, my career, and my general well-being. I needed to re-center, to find myself, and to step back from it all, so that I could get a better perspective on my situation.

I felt a harmonious energy from the very start of the meditation. But when I reached the direction/element of Fire, I wanted to run away. I felt a strong resistance to taking responsibility for the direction of my actions and movements.

I just wanted to let my arms drop and to cling on to something or someone. It was a really intense sensation. Tears started pouring down my face and I felt a great sense of relief. It was an experience of letting go that I felt throughout my whole being.

I did my best to follow the instructions and complete the movements and visualizations, and I discovered that I could channel my emotions. I have the ability to navigate the transitions in life with direction and intention. Memories resurfaced and I felt as though old wounds were healing. The pain had been buried, repressed, or denied because I didn't have the tools or support to complete these cycles. In the past, I've often been disappointed or frustrated, but I've carried on moving forward, ignoring everything that was building up within. During meditation, I became aware of all the pain and stress that had built up. I felt supported and relieved, and I was able to channel a new force that brought me comfort and a sense of peace.

I discovered that the element of Fire was related to self-esteem and self-confidence. This is an aspect I wanted to develop. Over the next few days, I noticed that I spoke more confidently and compassionately. My family appreciates my new way of expression, I have more confidence in my work relationships, and new doors have opened up for me. «

A few weeks later, Maryann decided to go on a trip: a dream trip she had been putting off for a very long time. She had opened up new paths on her journey with clarity and integrity.

A young man did the 28-day cycle to help him in his search for clarity

«While I was doing the Vortex of Energy Meditation on a daily basis, I patiently explored my thoughts, modes of functioning, choices, and values. The process took me through different stages. I managed to find a healthier point of reference. I felt as though my inner light was shining more clearly. Through meditation I was able to absorb my experiences wisely. I began to see the benefits of the discipline as I learned to stay in touch with my center and my truth throughout the day. I am now aware of the space of clarity that helps me find peace, and it is reflected in the way I am in harmony with my environment.

When the meditation is used counterclockwise it is like a cleansing process. It has helped me to reduce stress, and I feel more anchored and stable. I've gained the confidence to face the challenges in my path with more independence.

As I've gained a clearer understanding of this tool, I've been able to let go of behavior patterns that were unproductive or unbeneficial to my well-being. I feel stronger now faced with the influence of other people. Before, I wrongly thought that people expected certain behavior or responses from me, but it was just a projection of my own insecurities.

The process took place in harmony with those around me. When I did the Vortex of Energy Meditation for centering and aligning, I felt as though the energy flowed more freely throughout my whole being. I found it easier to recognize the times, thoughts, and distractions that make me deviate from my central point and those that allow me to stay in harmony with myself. I can come back more and more easily and consciously to my intention these days. One day, I was finding it difficult to stay focused and aware, because the experience I was having was bringing up a lot of frustration in me. I chose to let myself feel the emotion and channel it to express myself with clarity, and I avoided being carried away by the emotion into conflict with myself and those around me. I was aware that if I showed resistance, I developed conflictive emotions that were reflected in my behavior and my relationships with those around me!

Another time, I felt intense anger toward the Water Element during meditation. I wanted to shout and get rid of it, but instead I was able to accept it by inviting it to accompany me. It was a reconciliation with certain energies that I had always considered negative. I realized that if I was at peace

with my different emotions and experiences of being human, I inspired more peace among those around me too.

When I did the seven day Vortex of Energy Meditation in the form of expansion, I really felt my intention become stronger and clearer. I noticed that my thoughts and mind stayed focused all day after meditation. When I meditated first thing in the morning, my awareness and energy were stronger for the rest of the day. I was open and ready for new connections and opportunities. I felt lighter in my mind and throughout my whole being, which helped me to be more productive without getting stressed and to channel my energy more creatively. I also became more spontaneous and clearer in my decisions.

When I did the 28-day cycle, I began to realize the importance of regular discipline. My observations and awareness of sensations became clearer and clearer. The process has helped me assimilate daily experiences, establish my priorities, and direct my attention with more clarity during the day. I will continue doing this practice at least once a week.»

After experiencing the process for himself, he decided to train as a facilitator so he could develop the practice further and share the enriching experience with those around him. He is now a Licensed DHARMI Facilitator.

In Switzerland, a woman who was going through a difficult period in her personal relationships decided to attend some meditation sessions.

«…When I practiced the alignment stage in the Vortex of Energy Meditation, I found I was able to accept my reality more easily. I could face the situation with greater peace, tranquility, and compassion, and my worries didn't seem as bad.

I've realized that acceptance has increased my sense of responsibility for my life. It reminds me that I am my own destiny, and that it is up to me to manage my own reactions, thoughts, answers, and actions to the different situations in life.

I've noticed that I used to be very sensitive to the judgments and expectations of others. Now I'm also aware of my own needs and feelings. And I try to find a balance between the two. I've realized that there is abundance and space for everyone including myself. I'm more in touch with my feminine energy, my sensitivity, my intention, and my influence on this Earth and in our society.»

A person living in Peru asked for support dealing with a stressful situation. She did some DHARMI sessions on the internet. During these sessions, she was guided by a Licensed DHARMI Consultant through the Map to clarify her point of reference. After this stage of preparation and awakening her intention, she followed up with several Vortex of Energy Meditation sessions.

Claire* was experiencing a lot of conflict in her relationship with her partner, and she systematically victimized herself. She let herself be subject to aggressive judgments and emotional and verbal abuse.

«Yesterday, when I did the Meditation, I felt deeply grateful. I was aware of the sense of well-being that the practice and the routine has brought me. I attract different situations now. And I'm developing harmonious relationships with those around me. I realize that it's up to me to choose for things to go better and to act with positive intention. It is also up to me to direct my thoughts and actions in a healthy way. With this practice, I've been able to heal my wounds, regain a sense of harmony, and become stronger.»

Following this stage in her personal development process, Claire* has chosen to focus on a path that brings her a sense of well-being and harmony. She has done yoga training and is travelling toward new horizons.

Often our daily activities cause us a lot of stress, and it is difficult to find a space to re-center. If we do not take the time to reflect and review our position, our situation, our response mechanisms, and our behavior, we tend to deviate from our center.

Liz* was convinced she didn't have time to meditate because she was under too much pressure in her work and family life. The stress became more and more intense. As she didn't want to lose all perspective or get more physically sick from lack of sleep and worries, she decided to do a few sessions and try out a new method.

«I always thought that my stress and negative emotions came from outside circumstances. I thought that it was either out of my control or that I had to try and change other people and the outside world to improve it. By practicing what I've now learnt, I've come to realize that most of my stress came from my own interpretation of the world around me and from where I choose to focus my energy and attention.

Whenever there are big changes in my life, I choose to change my perspective, my tone of voice, and my movements now. I've gained confidence in myself and I have more energy. I'm more positive and relaxed now. It's interesting, because I actually control my life better now I've learnt how to let go.»

She continues with regular follow up DHARMI sessions online to re-center and clarify her perspective of herself and those around her.

I give regular seminars in the Jura, in Switzerland. On one occasion, I met a woman with very low self-esteem. She felt under constant pressure at work and continually accepted tasks that weren't her responsibility.

«During the presentation of the Vortex of Energy Meditation, I was immediately attracted by the method. By practicing every day, I've begun to feel a lot more energy, to feel much more grounded, and to experience great inner peace.

Day after day, I see the changes. It brings me positive energy and more self-confidence. My fears and worries have become a distant memory. I look to the future with clarity and serenity, and my heart is feeling more loving. My daily life is full of light and everything seems so much simpler and easier now. Whenever complications come into my life, I have more tools to handle it. My life has gained value and is full of opportunities for new encounters and a future rich in exchange and knowledge of my path.»

Following a first personal experience, she completed a 28-day process and a training course. She now continues to share her knowledge and to regularly guide people in the area through group and private meditation practices.

When we align the seven frequencies with positive intention, we are able to bring clarity to our communication. It is a way of creating a bridge—a link between our inner being, what we are at heart, and our surroundings.

A person who had difficulty expressing herself and making herself understood in her relationships with her partner, her family, and in daily life felt a real rift between herself and those around her. Communication with her partner was becoming increasingly difficult.

«I'm so happy to be taking part in your course. It makes me feel much more peaceful and relaxed, and I'm able to communicate better with my husband, without conflict. I can face daily life in the best possible conditions and with a positive outlook.»

By doing meditation, she has been able to center herself and take back control of her life in harmony and integrity, both in her relationship with her partner and in her communication with those around her.

As you have discovered reading the previous chapters, the magnetic field and our different elements, bodies, and frequencies are affected by, and retain the memory of trauma. It is possible to rebalance your physical, emotional, energetic, and mental bodies however. In this example, a woman shares her experience of going through rehabilitation following an accident. She sought to reconnect with the sensitivity of her physical body, and she also wanted to heal the trauma in her emotional and energetic bodies. She took part in a course lead by a facilitator in Switzerland.

«By doing regular active meditations, I've been able to feel the tingling in my hands better and the warmth and flow of energy through my body. I'm very strongly grounded, and I have the impression my feet are deeply rooted in the Earth. After the practice, I feel calm and relaxed.

I often experience strong emotions during meditation. I let go of a lot of things and then I feel lighter. Physically, even if the exercises are slow and simple, I feel like I've been doing gymnastics. I practice this meditation regularly. Since my accident, it's the thing that has done me the most good!»

This meditation is a very good complement to other therapies and rehabilitation processes. Through regular practice, subtle aspects that may have become unbalanced as a result of an accident or trauma can be restored.

Gil* had trouble finding his place in his social and family circle. He always felt like he didn't fit in. He started his process with regular DHARMI sessions to understand and learn how to manage this feeling of isolation.

«Since I began the Vortex of Energy Meditation, I have greater inner strength and integrity. A person who has always had a lot of influence on me and on my happiness, doesn't have so much influence now. My mind and my thoughts are clearer. I've found my inner strength, and it has helped me to take better control of my life.

I've managed to stop taking addictive substances. I realize that it still takes a lot of determination to maintain a healthy lifestyle. Creating new habits and healthy discipline has brought more harmony to my relationships.

When I forget to focus on my intention, I begin to lose confidence in myself again. I have learned that staying aware of my intention helps me act with clarity during the day. I feel more confident and focused.

The great revelation for me, was realizing that I didn't have to feel guilty about being so sensitive. I can accept my emotional limits now and take them into account. If I'm having a difficult day, I try to stay particularly aware of my behavior and relationships. In the past, I thought my sensitivity was the sign of a problem or a weakness. This reinforced my emotions and created a very intense internal conflict. By accepting myself as I am, I can approach life with greater confidence. My sensitivity has become a resource, and I try my best to listen to my intuition and emotional intelligence in my personal and work relationships.»

Some people are thrill seekers and have addictions that are very difficult to manage. But dependence on substances or relationships can cause stress and trauma. This person managed to improve his behavior patterns.

«The Vortex of Energy Meditation is powerful and harmonious. The practice has helped me gain confidence and awareness. It makes me feel more dynamic and I carry this feeling with me throughout the day. It fills me with healing energy. By being more attentive, I have become aware of the synchronicities in my life. I am able to stay centered, in alignment, and respectful of my needs and intuition. I've noticed that every morning after meditation, I have a sense of absolute well-being. I feel aligned with my destiny and it strengthens my energy. I feel more at peace in my daily life.

When I don't meditate, I notice that I'm less productive, and it makes me feel more vulnerable. At those times, I tend to be overwhelmed by dark thoughts and negative energy. I've noticed that regularly practicing this meditation has brought me a real sense of awareness, and I've been able to develop a healthier ego thanks to this awareness. It has awakened a new strength in me that encourages me to stay centered on what brings me happiness, and to take better care of myself and those around me.»

Sometimes we feel like we'll never be able to get rid of certain pain. We feel like we have neither the tools nor the knowledge to find an alternative in the healing process and our search for balance. This was Joanne's* experience, who suffered from chronic cystitis.

Joanne began taking part in regular meditation sessions to improve her sense of well-being and balance. She had already tried several methods to improve her chronic health condition, but in the end, she had become resigned to it, and learned to handle it as best she could. Her intention when she came to the sessions was mainly centered on finding comfort and harmony. During the meditation sessions and the following days, she felt a general sense of well-being and inner peace. Then, after practicing the meditation for several weeks, she realized she hadn't had cystitis for a long time. She chose to carry on with the sessions for several months. The alignment of her resonance with this intention freed her of a chronic symptom that she had suffered from for many years.

Some people choose to carry out the 28-day process. This is also one of the steps required for people who want to become a DHARMI Vortex of Energy Meditation facilitator. Below is the experience of Diana* who did his training in Miami, FL.

«When I do the Vortex of Energy Meditation counterclockwise, I feel the benefits almost immediately. This practice is particularly effective for releasing stress and negative emotions and changing bad habits. I used this meditation to improve my bad habits. The week I practiced it seven days in a row was particularly effective. It helped me gain clarity and focus my day in a healthy direction. It helped me create good habits like physical exercise, healthy food, yoga, and meditation. That week, the two nights I went out, I didn't feel the need to go beyond my limits. I find this meditation effective when I feel really stressed or overwhelmed by an emotion.

After completing the first part of the cleansing process, I moved on to the next stage doing this Meditation in a clockwise direction. The practice helps you focus and align yourself. I also did this meditation for seven consecutive days and after two days I already felt the benefits, feeling more at peace. I experienced a lot of synchronicities that week, and I bumped into people I hadn't seen in a long time by being in the right place at the right time. I also felt like life was less stressful and more peaceful. It was as though everything was in the right place at the right time. It helped me avoid destructive behavior patterns, because I stayed focused on a healthy lifestyle.

I put my whole heart into this practice. I really wanted to succeed in establishing a healthy lifestyle, which I had been trying to do on and off for several months. Every morning, after doing the Meditation, I felt my whole body vibrating and I experienced a surge of energy that lasted for the rest of the day. I found that healthier opportunities presented themselves to me and I went about what I had to do with more determination. That week, I worked intensively with my personal trainer and I also meditated a lot. I was more focused during the day and this helped me stay on a healthy path, in alignment with my intention.

The benefits of these Meditations can be felt within a few days if they are practiced consistently. But I don't have the discipline to practice them on a daily basis. I'm always looking for excuses to procrastinate. It's undeniable that when I practice these Meditations, they guide me towards a healthier lifestyle and allow me to make better decisions in life.»

Below are some observations shared by a woman who trained to become a facilitator in Switzerland:

«Since our Vortex of Energy Meditation seminar in January, I've found I'm much more attentive to the signs Life gives me. And the further I take it, the more I find it 'fun'. I'm more aligned, I feel more grounded, and I make decisions more easily. I have more confidence in life. I can open up and trust my personal gifts and potential. That's the approach I choose every day.

During my personal practice, over the first few days of clarification, I felt a space within me where I was able to release the powerful emotions I had been feeling after the loss of a friend. In certain places in my heart and throat, it was as though it were a little rusty. During the meditation and repetition of the movement I felt a sense of opening and harmonization.

Following my last two pregnancies, I had been suffering from fluid retention. But since I've been doing this meditation, I've eliminated a lot of it. I've lost four pounds without even changing my diet. I am waking up to the wisdom of my body. I give it space. For two or three years, I had also been suffering from knee pain. During the first few days of meditation, I could feel it very strongly. Centering reduced the pain, and now I don't feel it at all! This Meditation releases hidden fears from our bodies. I can go within, I feel safe, and I can just be me!

The following week, I focused on centering. I experienced a real sense of plenitude. I felt so peaceful. Everything was lighter, with a space of well-being. I could just relax and recharge.

After that experience, I did a week of reinforcement. A lot has changed since the seminar. Last Monday, I bumped into a girl from my childhood village who I hadn't seen for twenty years. She wanted to come and do a session with me. In the past, I hadn't been as open to the possibilities that could present themselves in daily life. Now I see the synchronicities, I'm spontaneous, alert, and I respond more actively to opportunities.

I've also been able to express my point of view to my children's teachers. I told them I wanted to support my child's creativity, whereas in the past, with my first child, I let the expectations and rules of a linear system take precedence over my child's need for expression and fulfillment. I have more confidence in myself and communicate more clearly now, so everything went well.

I tend to force things and then not follow them through. I'm learning to respect myself. Before, I often had headaches, but now the back of my head feels clearer. I have a greater sense of self-esteem, and I have the energy to follow my path—freeing up and organizing space creates space for real action. My feet are grounded.

I did a 28-day cycle. Now I try to do the Meditation twice a week in addition to the courses I run myself. Sometimes I come back to past situations in order to reenergize myself. Other times, I follow the course of my day. That helps me a lot. I've also noticed that if I'm able to do the Meditation in the morning, my day is much calmer and more centered, and I eat more healthily, even if that isn't the easiest time for me.»

This facilitator runs guided meditation sessions for several participants. Here, she shares some of her experiences.

«Some participants open up to new experiences without ever having meditated or done yoga before. One woman wanted to come and try the Vortex of Energy Meditation. She had received an invitation that had inspired confidence in her and awakened her curiosity. When she joined us for her first session, she had never felt her energy before and she found it fascinating. She had been suffering from shoulder pain for several weeks at the time, and two days later the pain was gone.

Her experience is interesting. This woman opened up very quickly to the synchronicities in life and she is now trying to develop her awareness. Every Monday, she arrives a little early and shares her latest experience with me and tells me what she has become aware of. She always enjoys coming to the practice. She is more peaceful and centered now. I've noticed a real difference in her behavior and expression.

Martin* opened up on the very first Meditation experience

The movement involved in this Meditation helped him channel his thoughts and brought him back to the essentials, in a more serene space with himself and those around him. He has noticed a lot of changes, especially in his relationship with his partner. He also feels more grounded with his teenage daughter. He attends regular classes. He re-centers himself to complete certain cycles, clarify his thoughts, and gain perspective, while recharging himself with positive energy.

Martin atteded sessions throughout February, and he showed real motivation and pleasure in coming. He has understood that he can really influence what happens around him. He's evolved in a truly wonderful way. He's realized that we become and we experience what we create, perceive, and project.

Some people notice they feel better and sleep more deeply than before. Others have clearer perspective or find a solution to a «problem». They find their joy and enthusiasm in life again.

The most common response among participants when describing what they feel is «tranquility and inner peace after aligning their seven frequencies.» The observations become subtler when this alignment and centering is performed regularly. The practice becomes a journey of awakening, sensitivity, and perception of the seven voices.

Morgane was struggling to regain the full movement in her shoulder after an accident a few years back. The physical pain had gone, and her body had recovered, but her movements still reflected the emotional trauma of pain. It was like a resistance, a spontaneous reaction that appeared at certain times and under certain circumstances. She decided to do a 28-day cycle to complete the healing process. She did all the dynamic Meditations in group sessions, three times a week. On the other days, she focused on visualization and some basic strategic movements. After three or four days, she noticed a real difference and so she continued with it. She deepened the process to release the hidden fears behind the memory of the accident, as well as certain emotions, judgments, and feelings that she hadn't been able to acknowledge or absorb. As a result of this cycle, she developed greater self-esteem, and she began to express herself with more compassion and harmony.

Examples - Experiences - Students & Practitioners

Below I share two examples. Both are the experiences of people who did the Vortex of Energy Meditation to support their well-being and find balance in a time of transition in their life.

In this first example, Kim was facing a difficult time in her family. Her friend recommended she try a holistic approach before using a more intrusive method to face the situation and the state of depression that it was triggering in her.

Kim had just received the news from her husband that he wanted a separation followed by a divorce. They have been married for more than eight years and been through many different challenges during their relationship. Until now, they had been able to overcome many situations of conflict, focusing on better times, and nurturing family quality time to maintain the structure together, for each other and their children. They had different values that were causing strong, fundamental imbalances and conflicts in their relationship.

Kim felt a lot of anger and deep sadness. The pain was so profound that she didn't have any appetite and couldn't sleep. We took into consideration her feelings and beliefs that were in direct connection with this deep pain. She noticed that her own expectations were making the process even more difficult and hurtful. She also became aware that her resistance and a certain level of denial was not helping her anymore. I use the word "anymore" on purpose. As we spoke, she noticed that some level of denial had helped her in the past. This behavior and choice of perspective had helped her to keep the family together. Yet now, too many factors had come up to the surface to continue to deny the truth. It was time to accept and face a hurtful reality.

We began with a Vortex of Energy Meditation counter-clockwise. This practice helped her to accept and have more compassion with her beliefs even when they caused her pain. She also began to gain some distance from her pain-body response. As we were passing through the Meditation facing all seven frequencies, she noticed the most resistance in the Water Element. It was an overwhelming sensation filled with emotions that were difficult to channel. That experience gave her tools and clarity. It helped her to forgive and practice compassion. She could channel her own emotions with more leadership and direction.

At the foundation or base, she experienced a surprising sensation of support and confidence. It gave her a strength that was new and foreign to her. She felt a sense of clearing and release, together with the support to contain her emotions and direct her actions and life.

In the following days, she noticed a distance from the trauma and began to deal with the situation with more harmony. For the first seven days, she did the Vortex of Energy Meditation counterclockwise. It was a daily routine, performed at a same time. It had been given to her as a healthy ritual, full of healing and nurturing intention.

Over the first three days, Kim encountered a lot of pain and resistance. Many flashbacks came to her awareness. It was as if everything began to make sense. She and her husband had completed a cycle and their relationship was coming to an end. Their paths needed space in order to grow with respect and harmony. They had both grown out of love and began to develop a love that was not a romantic "couple" love anymore. It was a new dimension with which she began to make peace. This understanding gave her the space to release judgment and open a new perspective.

After completing seven days of the Clearing Form, she entered the Alignment Form. Many truths appeared in her consciousness, as well as in her surroundings and relationships. This process brought clarity to her communication. It brought to light some aspects that she had repressed. Some truths confirming some of her apprehension came to the surface. The process was mind-blowing, yet she found the strength to see the reality as she continued her daily practice.

The Alignment and Centering Form has been key for her to nurture her values and find clarity. She began to gain self-respect and see her value as something she could be proud of and honor as a woman. This level of acceptance of her values brought her closer to her children. Their relationship became more harmonious and authentic, honoring everyone's space to process the situation their own way.

Then, came the time to begin the clockwise version of the Vortex of Energy Meditation. She felt that it wasn't the time to move on yet, to rebuild and nurture a new perspective. Kim's fear was holding her back as she was trying to attach onto what was familiar. We recognized the resistance and took into consideration her own rhythm to take the next step with prudence and care, when she was ready. In this situation in her life, it was key not to overextend, but rather to act with clarity and healthy values.

Her husband was moving out. He had already found another place to live. The process of separation was really happening this time. They had to explain it to the children and answer questions from all directions.

Practicing the Vortex of Energy Meditation clockwise brought a sense of strength and balance. It helped her to fill the void with intention and nurturing thoughts and actions towards herself, her children and their new reality. Her creative potential was awakening. She was exploring a new perspective and building up a healthy intention in the emptiness. Everything was happening so fast. This form of the Vortex of Energy Meditation cycle provided her with tools to channel her emotions daily and to carry out actions creatively. It was a daily practice to solidify her intention and honor her well-being. She became emotionally stronger. She was restructuring, yet reorganizing basic aspects in her organization with the children, home and school, as well as the administrative aspects that she had to face.

Digesting our life's experiences is key to allowing us to fully integrate the learning process. For the last seven days Kim had been focused on a time to integrate and assimilate. That time had been dedicated to settling, resting, and being in a space of non-doing, while taking care of priorities. Non-doing is an art, one in which we don't bring or initiate anything new, rather just letting whatever is going to happen, happen and managing what is in the present experience. This period gave her the space and time to care for her foundations and basic needs before reacting too quickly trying to compensate for anything she lacked. Only with such a healthy grounding can we grow. Kim was surprised by the integrity in her comprehension, integration and healing process. We began another 28-day cycle to move into the next step in this profound life transition.

Now, a few months later, she and her husband's relationship reflects a mutual respect, supporting the well-being of their children and each other's evolution. It has been a transition made with healthy values.

In this second example, Ronald contacted me at a moment in his life, when he had to make an important decision. He had begun to develop a project, yet he noticed that many distractions were inhibiting his success. Should he focus and pursue this direction, or let go and head in a brand-new direction?

We noticed that it had been a vicious circle that he experienced in many situations in his life. He would initiate a project yet he wouldn't follow it through. It was more comfortable for him to keep the doors open and stay in one place, without walking through any of those openings. It came from a fear of failure, fear of making a mistake, fear of commitment—whatever it was called, it was all fear. What had to be considered was how he faced, experienced and channeled his fears.

He noticed that he resisted that fearful emotion. He tried to repress fear judging that it wasn't manly to feel afraid. The core belief "I shouldn't" is directly connected to the emotion of fear. When fear came up in Ronald, resistance came too, together with the belief that he shouldn't do anything—taking no step seemed the safest option. This vicious circle had affected him in many different situations in his life.

We began with a Vortex of Energy Meditation counterclockwise. That experience gave him time, space and clarity. He noticed how attached he was to certain behavior and that he could access a potential and a strength that he had repressed on many occasions. He had been seeing things as black or white, all or nothing. The space in between was unexplored.

During the Meditation, he began to find a state of peace. Yet, as we reached the Fire Element's direction, he felt a strong anxiety. He lost focus and wanted to give in. The challenge of measuring and leading his actions and his inner fire was unpleasant. It was overwhelming and uncomfortable. We passed through that resistance. We continued the Meditation to link all seven directions. In the following days, he was more aware of his responses and defense mechanisms. He began to clarify healthy boundaries with his surroundings.

It was difficult for Ronald to do the Vortex of Energy Meditation daily. Yet, his determination to explore this new space supported him to do a visualization of the Meditation on the days he didn't do it actively and completely. He noticed that he had more space and possibilities around him than he thought. He opened himself up to different options, releasing attachments and overly-high expectations that couldn't be immediately fulfilled.

In the first part of the counterclockwise form, he found a new space and more flexibility. He focused on those qualities for the Centering version. During that time of alignment, he accepted a new opportunity and continued his own project on the side. He could organize his time and began to nurture healthy relationships. He became more aware and learned to accept his journey, being more present and patient through daily experiences, rather than constantly focusing on goals or expectations.

Ronald found new ways to approach his vision and chose to give it a chance. When he began the Expansion form, he noticed an impatience rising in him. He wanted to rush the movements and experience. He felt overwhelmed by an inner strength and profound sensations. He was aware of some impulsive behaviors he had engaged in previously. At that part of the cycle, he noticed that his main fear concerned his own force. He became aware that he was scared of improperly channeling or directing his strength and potential. This level of consciousness brought to the surface some memories from his childhood, when his father had been aggressive towards him and his mother. It brought back the fear of a masculine power that was not manageable and so out of control.

He became aware of that inner strength and clarified an intention in which it could be a positive asset for him. His intention appeared to be to lead with patience and clarity, taking one step at a time. This intention inspired him to accept that inner potential and to cultivate it. So, we began to practice the form of Expansion of the Vortex of Energy Meditation.

Day after day, he became more familiar with that inner potential and began to channel it with harmony and confidence. Through the days, he was more focused and noticed that his presence was having a new impact on his surroundings. Some people began to approach him with more respect. He was responding with more clarity, leading the conversation with intention and inspiration.

When he completed that form, and entered in a space of integration, he chose to continue to meditate daily. It became a routine that reminded him to stay mindful and attentive to himself and others around him.

We continued the journey using the DHARMI Method to support his progress and the manifestation of his vision. A few months later, his project was taking form and showing the first signs of prosperity, giving Ronald a sense of satisfaction and success. He was still working at another stable job, but devoting only part of his time was now enough for him to have a balanced and prosperous life.

Author's Testimony: Christelle Chopard

«I make sure I center myself regularly and balance my seven frequencies. This discipline contributes to my well-being and keeps me in a space of compassion throughout the day.

One day, I trapped a nerve while swimming and it created a lot of inflammation. I couldn't open the door or touch my right shoulder with my left hand. The pain was so intense I could hardly sleep at night, and I was considering going to the hospital to find out what was happening. But I decided to focus on the holistic DHARMI approach and the Vortex of Energy Meditation first. I set myself a pain threshold and a time limit of one week. If things hadn't improved by the end of the week, I would go and see a doctor.

During one of my two daily sessions, there was a series of very subtle and deep crunches in my neck, shoulder, and even in the space between my throat and neck. These crunches were accompanied by a series of flashbacks. After that, I felt as though everything was settling back into place. Two days later, I was able to resume my yoga practice and use my arm as normal.

It is my own experiences that have inspired me to share this methodology to support the well-being, enrichment, and personal and professional development of those around me.»

GLOSSARY

Agape: Unconditional love in Greek.

Apana: Downward-flowing energy.

Askasha: The omnipresent existence that pervades all things.

Ayurveda: The «science of life», a holistic medical approach dating back to the Vedic civilization that is still influential today. A traditional form of Indian medicine.

Bandha: A masculine Sanskrit term meaning the act of linking, a bond, link, attachment, or chain. Used in the Vortex of Energy to mean a lock.

DHARMI® Method: Created by Christelle Chopard, this Method for holistic stress management is designed to support well-being in the community. It is a Map for self and professional development. It combines teachings from the six continents and is a guide in daily life. The Method involves three paths. The first path is based on the Cycle of Evolution, the second on the Vortex of Energy, and the third on the Cycle of Energy. These three paths complement each other to support a complete and holistic development process. However, each path can also be used independently.

Chakras: A Sanskrit term meaning wheel or disk; spiritual centers or connecting points for the energy channels in the human body. There are seven main chakras. Each chakra is an energy vortex.

Cycle of Evolution: A holistic and integral portal involving five stages for the release of stress and conditioning. The process allows you to discover your talents, qualities, and true potential in a space of clarification, and to find your true expression.

(Reference: the book «Cycle of Evolution - Five steps to navigate life transitions with mindfulness»).

Cycle of Energy: A holistic approach based on the Five Elements that supports the process of manifesting inspiration. The stages of this cycle are part of an integral method to identify the necessary resources, values, and healthy relationships in a space of motivation, inspiration, and clear reflection. The process allows for the holistic clarification needed to make conscious decisions and develop a balanced lifestyle.

(Reference: «Elements on the Journey»).

Dantians: Energy centers that store and generate Qi (life force energy) in the body. Places where life force energy is produced, accumulated, and preserved.

Dharma: The collection of all the social, political, family, personal, natural, and cosmic norms and laws. The universal law. The teachings that support a path of truth and healthy values.

DHARMI®: Word, service-trademark registered by Christelle Chopard to define her method based on the Five Elements and Seven Frequencies, which supports the process of manifesting an intention with compassion and wisdom. It involves a sacred Map that facilitates the transition from karma (experience) to dharma (integration and wisdom). Ref: DHARMI Method mentioned above. Also, DHARMI-YOGA® and other approaches based on the philosophy and concept of the Five Elements and Seven Frequencies for holistic self-development are included below this same service-trademark.

Eros: Romantic love, special chemistry, alchemy in Greek.

Filia: Love between friends, colleagues, and people who share common interests and visions in Greek.

Gunas: A quality or property. The three main qualities that interact together to produce all forms of «creation». The gunas are divided into three essential substances:

Sattva: purity and truth;

Rajas: energy, passion, strength, and desire;

Tamas: obscurity, darkness, heaviness, and inertia.

These three gunas are independent, but are in endless interaction in different proportions in nature. Their reciprocal action controls all evolution of matter.

Hexagram: From the Greek: hexa meaning six and gram meaning letter or writing; a geometrical figure representing the soft and the firm, the dark and the light, the weak and the strong, the yin and the yang.

Hopi: The Hopi are part of the Amerindian group of the Native American Pueblo Peoples, neighbors of the Apaches, Navajos, Tohono O'odham people, and Zuñis. The Hopi live in northeastern Arizona, in the very arid Four Corners region.

Ida Inipi: Ida is one of the three tubes, the main vessels of the nadis, energy channels that circulate in our bodies. Ida is the feminine force and is white.

The Inipi is a kind of round tent or hut, created for a sacred purification and healing ceremony. It is traditionally practiced and used by native American peoples.

Jalandhara bandha: Jalandhara bandha is the bandha, link, or lock that connects the elements of Fire and Air. It is located in the area of the throat.

Kalachakra: Kalachakra means time-cycle or wheel of time. The Tibetan mandala.

Karma: In Sanskrit: action in all its forms, in a more religious sense, ritual action. It is also the cycle of cause and effect related to the existence of sentient beings in duality.

Lakota: A native American tribe. Part of the Sioux people. The Lakota live in North and South Dakota (USA) as well as in Canada. We find Lakotas also in some areas of Mexico and South America when they travel for specific ceremonies.

Mandala: A Sanskrit term meaning circle, and by extension, sphere, environment, or community. In Buddhism, it is mostly used for meditation. The diagram is always filled with symbols and may be associated with a divinity. Mandala symbolizes life creation from the source towards expansion and manifestation.

Mantra: A dictum or maxim; a sacred hymn, mystical phrase, or magical incantation. A condensed utterance consisting of one or a series of repeated syllables following a certain rhythm for meditation or religious purposes. It can also be a prayer, an affirmation, or a thought that one wishes to strengthen and integrate in its vibration by continually repeating it (108 times in Buddhist philosophy).

Merkaba: A Hebrew term meaning cart (from the root R-K-B meaning "to ride"). It is one of the oldest themes of Jewish mysticism, and allows the mystic to contemplate the celestial throne.

Mula bandha: The «Muladhara Lock» or the bond of the «root chakra», the first chakra, located at the base of the spine. It is related to the foundations of human life (life force or vital energy) and our primordial energies of survival, the need for security, the relationship with material things and the concrete aspects of life, sexuality, the relationship with the Earth, and roots. It is also related to physical and mental balance.

Nadi: Tube, channel, vessel; a nadi is an energy channel that runs up along the main chakras, close to the spine. There are three main nadis, which each carry a specific energy: the masculine (Pingala), the feminine (Ida) and the neutral (Sushumna), somewhat like electricity. According to certain traditions, there are 72,000 channels in the human body, comparable to the meridians in acupuncture. The nadis are the channels through which the energies of the subtle body circulate, namely the vital energy called «prana». They are related to the nervous system and stem from the chakras which they are closely related to.

Pacha Mama: The Mother Earth. Known as Gaia in other philosophies.

Pingala: One of the three nadi channels, together with Ida and Sushumna, which cross the chakras from the base of the trunk to the crown of the head, allowing energy to pass and thus to create light within the chakras.

Prana: The Sanskrit term for Qi is life force energy. It is directly related to the breath. An ascending energy.

Qigong: Traditional Chinese gymnastics and the science of breathing based on knowledge and control of our life force energy, combining slow movements, breathing exercises, and concentration. Qi means vital energy and Gong means activation. Qigong means activation of the vital energy.

Qi or Chi: The vital energy or life force energy that regulates the ebb and flow of vitality in all things. It is called lung in Tibetan, prana in Sanskrit, and ki in Japanese. Aristotle referred to it when he spoke of the souls of energy that exist in all of nature, where they can be found in the form of a sign.

Raja: One of the three gunas. The active essence of force and desire, the principle of movement, intensity.

Rajastic: Movement and passion.

Sattvic: Goodness, the state of being alert, centered, and awakened but serene.

Storge: Familial love, sacrifice, and a sense of duty in Greek.

Sushumna: A Sanskrit term: the central psychic path. The central channel. One of the three energy channels (nadis).

Sweat Lodge: A sweat lodge is an important ritual in Amerindian tradition and spirituality. The sweat lodge is the Inipi mentioned above.

Tai chi: An internal Chinese martial art practiced in two dimensions for combat and for health benefits.

Tamas: One of the three gunas in Samkhya philosophy. Inertia, resistance to action, passivity.

Tantra: Tantra is a set of practices that supports the development of consciousness.

Taoism: A teaching of the path. A philosophy and a religion,one of the three pillars of Chinese thought together with Confucianism and Buddhism, based on the existence of an original principle at the origin of all things, known as «Tao».

Temazcal: A Temazcal is a ceremony that includes a kind of sweat lodge native to the pre-Hispanic civilizations of Central America. A native American term for sweat lodge.

Torus: A three dimensional, spherical geometric figure resembling a donut. A circle with a hollow used in sacred geometry. Its evolutionary form creates a sphere.

Tsampa: The Tibetan name for roasted barley flour. The traditional staple foodstuff in Tibet.

Uddiyanna bandha: The abdominal lock (Bandha). Uddiyana means "upwards" and Bandha means "lock".

Vortex: The main energy vortexes are positioned on the chakras traditionally represented on the front of the body.

DHARMI Vortex of Energy Meditation: A meditation practice that activates the release of stress at the emotional, psychological, physical, and energetic levels and balances the Seven Frequencies.

This active Meditation helps us to clarify the five fundamental energies: Earth, Water, Fire, Air, and Ether, and the Seven Frequencies. The practice reinforces the electromagnetic field and balances resonance with intention. Created by Christelle

Chopard, it combines different practices that she studied and experimented with during her research.

(Reference: this book)

Yang: Yang represents, among other things, the masculine, the sun, brightness, heat, plenitude, and momentum. In Chinese philosophy, yin and yang are two complementary forces found in all aspects of life and the universe. This notion of complementarity is traditional to Oriental thought, which more readily thinks of duality in terms of complementarity.

Yantra: A Yantra is a diagram from the Hindu tradition used as an aid in meditation. Yantras reflect different concepts and aspects of life.

Yin: Yin refers to the feminine, the moon, darkness, freshness, emptiness, and receptivity. In Chinese philosophy, yin and yang are two complementary forces found in all aspects of life and the universe. This notion of complementarity is traditional to Oriental thought, which more readily thinks of duality in terms of complementarity.

We often must face resistance in one of our voices, or we are destabilized by the weakness of another voice. We can only enjoy the benefits of this meditation when we commit ourselves willingly and fully to each of the frequencies. If our movements are too jerky, if our thoughts are distracted, or if our intention is not clear, the process will not allow for the energetic opening and alignment that you could experience by carrying out this active Meditation with clarity, direction, and awareness. I therefore emphasize the importance of practicing the sessions with a certified facilitator by attending one of their courses or doing sessions on the internet.

More and more people are taking the training course and becoming facilitators, allowing for more direct and regular exchanges in many different locations. It is also possible to take a course online or to organize a seminar in your area if there is not yet a certified Vortex of Energy Meditation Facilitator near you.

To support your personal development process, the Map includes three paths. There is a book for each of the paths, and you can find more information at: www.dharmi.com

The book, **"Cycle of Evolution"** explains the steps required to bring clarity to your point of reference. This can open up new doors, perspectives, and possibilities on your path.

The book about the Cycle of Energy, **"Elements on the Journey"**, offers many examples of how the Elements complement each other to bring about healthy and harmonious development.

Made in the USA
Middletown, DE
10 October 2022